Praise for *From Triggere*

"Drawing on a lifetime's experience as a couple therapist and relationship coach, Susan Campbell shows how to recognize when we are triggered and explore what lies behind it. She presents straightforward, practical ways to return to a calmer state of mind — and does so with kindness, compassion, clarity, and wisdom. Anyone who gets triggered from time to time — and that's just about all of us — should read this book. And keep it handy for when we find ourselves caught in some emotional reaction."

— **Peter Russell**, author of *Letting Go of Nothing*
and *From Science to God*

"Well written and crystal-clear, this book offers simple tools for noticing when we've been hijacked by our lizard brain and replacing our automatic reactions with responses that help us feel more connected to ourselves, each other, and our world."

— **John Amodeo, PhD**, author of *Dancing with Fire*

"Dr. Campbell once again masterfully guides us all toward being more self-aware, compassionate, and skillful in communicating with others and creating authentic, healthy relationships. In *From Triggered to Tranquil*, she shows you how to quickly catch emotional reactivity, compassionately calm yourself, and speak with effective honesty without blame. I will recommend this book to all my clients."

— **Dr. Aziz Gazipura**, bestselling author of *Not Nice*

"A great and practical set of skillful tools for wise and compassionate living."

— **Jack Kornfield**, author of *A Path with Heart*

"Susan Campbell has done it. Most self-help books leave the reader on the outside, looking in. You understand what the author is saying, but their words don't actually ignite transformation. This book does the opposite. It invites you right into the heart of your own unique experience. You feel deeply seen and genuinely understood. And you are offered tools and techniques that are immediately useful in your relational life. You don't just make sense of your patterns; you actually begin to transform them. For anyone who wants to find peace with their triggers, this accessible and comforting book is a must-read. I loved it."

— **Jeff Brown**, author of *Soulshaping* and *Grounded Spirituality*

"It sometimes seems difficult to understand why we react the way we do — why we get upset at things that seem small or we shut down when someone uses the wrong word. Susan Campbell beautifully answers the question 'Why do we get triggered, and what can we do about it?' with clear and simple strategies for getting back on track. I've been a connection teacher for over a decade, and this book taught me new language, tools, and techniques. I am already applying them in my practice and my life!"

— **Sara Ness**, founder and CEO of Authentic Revolution

"In *From Triggered to Tranquil*, Susan Campbell shows how self-knowledge leads to self-actualization. Once you understand who you are and how you became that way, you can reframe difficult situations, change the narrative, and rewrite the script of your life."

— **Jack Canfield**, coauthor of the Chicken Soup for the Soul® series and *The Success Principles*™

From Triggered to Tranquil

Also by Susan Campbell, PhD

Beyond the Power Struggle

The Couple's Journey

Earth Community

Expanding Your Teaching Potential

The Everything Great Sex Book
(coauthored by Suzie Heumann)

Five-Minute Relationship Repair
(coauthored by John Grey, PhD)

From Chaos to Confidence

Getting Real

Saying What's Real

Truth in Dating

From Triggered to Tranquil

How Self-Compassion and Mindful Presence Can Transform Relationship Conflicts and Heal Childhood Wounds

Susan Campbell, PhD

New World Library
Novato, California

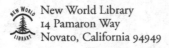 New World Library
14 Pamaron Way
Novato, California 94949

The material in this book is intended for education. No expressed or implied guarantee of the effects of the use of the recommendations can be given or liability taken.

Text design by Tona Pearce Myers

Library of Congress Cataloging-in-Publication Data

Names: Campbell, Susan M., date, author.
Title: From triggered to tranquil : how self-compassion and mindful presence can transform relationship conflicts and heal childhood wounds / Susan Campbell, PhD.
Description: Novato, California : New World Library, [2021] | Summary: "A self-help guide for anyone who has ever become upset, defensive, numb, or disoriented by another person's behavior. The author helps readers understand their emotional triggers, reframe the situation, and find constructive ways of coping. Includes exercises and practices"-- Provided by publisher.
Identifiers: LCCN 2021022081 (print) | LCCN 2021022082 (ebook) | ISBN 9781608687404 (paperback) | ISBN 9781608687411 (epub)
Subjects: LCSH: Adjustment (Psychology) | Emotions. | Interpersonal conflict. | Self-acceptance.
Classification: LCC BF335 .C355 2021 (print) | LCC BF335 (ebook) | DDC 155.2/4--dc23
LC record available at https://lccn.loc.gov/2021022081
LC ebook record available at https://lccn.loc.gov/2021022082

First printing, August 2021
ISBN 978-1-60868-740-4
Ebook ISBN 978-1-60868-741-1
Printed in Canada

 New World Library is proud to be a Gold Certified Environmentally Responsible Publisher. Publisher certification awarded by Green Press Initiative.

10   9   8   7   6   5   4   3   2

Contents

Introduction

Triggers, Trauma, and Trigger Work

The Path to Self-Healing

Our unprocessed emotional wounds and the re-actions that arise from them are what make us go to war, blow up at our children, get hostile on the freeways, hit "send" on that email rant, walk out of meetings, argue with our loved ones, and make short-sighted decisions.

This book is a self-help guide for anyone who has ever gotten emotionally reactive, defensive, shut down, or overwhelmed in an adult relationship or group. That includes almost everyone. The hurts and disappointments that we suffer in childhood often leave lasting scars with respect to our inner sense of safety and security. These insecurities will show up later in our adult relationships in the form of trigger reactions. But this is not necessarily a bad thing. In this book, you will learn how to work with such reactions in a way that brings healing to your childhood wounds, deeper connections with others, and an expanded sense of what it means to be human.

You may be one of those people who have been told you're too sensitive or too much, so you already suspect you need healing around this issue. Or you may not have big, expressive reactions to things; you may be someone who keeps upset feelings and disappointments to yourself. Or perhaps you're pretty even-tempered, only getting flustered when someone comes at you aggressively, so you might think you just need some tips for dealing with difficult people. But even if someone rarely gets triggered, there is a good chance that they still have emotional wounds waiting in the shadows to become activated in a future relationship.

This book teaches how to catch and calm trigger reactions quickly so we can get back to being present and resourceful. The underlying premise is that we can heal emotional wounds that originate in childhood, but to do so involves what I call *trigger work*. The starting point for this work is the experience of getting triggered into some version of fight, flight, or freeze — which may involve angry feelings, a tight chest, the urge to hide, and so on. Once we notice or catch such reactions, then we can learn how to explore our fears, hurts, and other difficult feelings. In time, this helps us view painful experiences from a wider perspective and realize that experiencing pain or fear does not mean there's something wrong with us. In fact, painful emotions can be a portal to a deeper understanding of life and our relationship to it.

To reinforce key concepts, each chapter begins with an italicized one- or two-sentence excerpt from that chapter. Most of the exercises in this book can be done on your own — even if the reactions in question were triggered by other people.

The chapters in part 2 describe specific ways to apply these practices in your relationships with intimate partners, friends, children, coworkers, groups, and even strangers.

Many of the exercises ask that you recall memories of past or recent trigger reactions and notice the feelings, sensations, and thoughts that come up. This repetition is important. Ideally, you will become so well-practiced at dealing with trigger reactions that you learn to take such reactions in stride. Practicing any new skill builds confidence, and so it is with the skill of working with trigger reactions.

The Root of Most Human Conflict

I got into the field of psychotherapy so I could help people live happier, more fulfilling lives. I have been doing this work for fifty-five years. And I believe I have discovered the root of most human unhappiness, conflict, and dysfunction: It is the fact that we do not know how to accept and work with painful emotions and trigger reactions, so we project the cause of our reactions onto others, thus creating needless conflict and misguided action. If we could learn how to accept and work with the painful realities of our lives — instead of blaming, scapegoating, denying, and repressing — this world would be a saner, safer, friendlier place. Our unprocessed emotional wounds and the reactions that arise from them are what make us go to war, blow up at our children, get hostile on the freeways, hit "send" on that email rant, walk out of meetings, argue with our loved ones, and make short-sighted decisions. Our invisible or inner trigger reactions are what make us too shy to ask for a date, afraid to speak up for ourselves at work, walk on eggshells with our spouse, and freeze up when speaking to groups.

We get triggered far more often than we realize. When we are in this state, our decisions come from the wrong part of our brain — the primitive lizard part — instead of the more evolved prefrontal cortex that is capable of seeing longer-term consequences and more than one point of view. So we need to learn how to get untriggered and regain access to our higher brain functioning before tackling whatever external problem we are facing.

When we get triggered, our nervous system quickly releases strong neurochemicals like adrenaline (the activating hormone) and cortisol (the stress hormone) that cause us to react automatically, without realistic awareness of our full range of options. We are blind to the actual possibilities available to us. Creative problem-solving goes out the window. Behavior becomes automatic, rigid, patterned, and stereotyped. We regress to the least resourceful version of ourselves — sort of like a cornered animal.

But it's not our fault. We are not bad or weak for getting triggered. And if another person triggers us, it's not their fault, either. Getting triggered is a survival mechanism that is built into our nervous system. We all need to learn to deal with getting triggered. We are born with this survival alarm mechanism in the amygdala area of the brain. This alarm system originally developed to alert our animal ancestors to potential physical danger in the world around them. It is always scanning for danger. And to ensure physical survival, it is wired to react quickly — to act first and think later. In our primitive ancestry, when saber-toothed tigers or other predators were a real threat, the brain evolved to have instantaneous reactions of fight, flight, or freeze to anything that even remotely resembled a predator. In primitive times, it was an evolutionary advantage to react instinctively, without taking time to assess, "Is this a real danger or a false alarm?"

Interpersonal "Dangers" Feel Dangerous, Too

In these modern times, we are not in danger of a tiger jumping out at us from the next bush. Nowadays, our survival alarm system is mostly scanning for a different kind of danger — the danger we feel when there is (or seems to be) a threat to something else that we regard as vital for our survival. These things can include:

- our connection with someone special whom we depend on
- approval or acceptance from others
- our self-image, such as being seen as competent, strong, good, honest, smart, right, trustworthy, and so on
- our financial security
- our sense of inclusion or belonging in a group

Of course, the world still contains threats to our physical well-being — we can get triggered by a reckless driver on the highway or when we have to wait too long for medical attention in the ER. This book does not focus primarily on these types of physical dangers — except in instances where a shock trauma, such as being hit by a drunk driver, restimulates an earlier developmental trauma, such as where the child was beaten by a drunk parent or an irresponsible older sibling. Such physical traumas can leave lasting emotional scars — especially if the child did not have anyone to talk to or to get comfort from after an incident. No matter how your triggers originated, the practices in this book will help you integrate those unprocessed experiences and complete the unfinished emotional business associated with them.

It is possible to learn to navigate trigger reactions without falling automatically into fight-flight-freeze. That's the job of our higher brain centers — our frontal and prefrontal cortex. Over the course of evolution, humans developed these higher brain centers that can modify the quick reactivity of the middle and lower brain centers. The higher brain has the capacity to remind us that our boss's flat voice tone does not necessarily mean disapproval — even though our instinctive reaction is to feel protective or defensive. The cortex also makes self-witnessing possible — the ability to step back from being enmeshed with our reactivity and to consciously choose a response that fits the actual situation. While we may always be triggered, and experience an instantaneous defensive reaction, when we hear a critical tone of voice, we can learn to catch and interrupt this reaction as soon as it begins.

Life wants us to learn from experience, to develop, to heal, and to evolve into higher states of being. And it gives us everything we need to heal ourselves and evolve. Our job is to pay attention, to be aware, to be present to the actuality of each moment. We can't learn from experience when we're on automatic and thus unable to see, hear, and feel what is actually going on. If we are going to learn to master our trigger reactions, we have to learn to slow things down.

Trigger Reactions Can Foster Self-Knowledge

My life's work is dedicated to helping people slow down and pay attention — so we can catch and halt those automatic reactions and take action with awareness of our full range of choices. Slow down and catch that automatic tendency to hear disagreement as criticism. Slow down and notice that impatient need to get a commitment from the person you're dating. Slow down that impulse to walk out in the middle of an argument or to give up or feign agreement in order to keep the peace.

Learning to recognize your trigger reactions is the starting point for this journey. Trigger reactions are portals into the human unconscious. They help us see and understand why we do many of the things we do — especially the things that, at first glance, appear self-defeating. For instance, when we become hostile when someone doesn't want to be romantic, or we get defensive when a professor gives critical feedback on an assignment.

Your trigger reactions can be the doorway to understanding and embodying a much bigger life process that I like to call *whole-making*. As I see it, life itself is about whole-making — integrating the various parts of a system into increasingly interrelated wholes. Our trigger reactions help us see aspects of ourselves that we may be unaware of. As we explore these reactions, we discover parts of ourselves that have been denied, abandoned, or repressed. This is the realm of the human unconscious that psychologists call our *shadow*. As we enter through this portal, we encounter forgotten hurts and disappointments, unmet childhood needs, protective personality habits that we adopted to keep us safe, beliefs that help us make sense of things we don't understand, and ideas about ourselves and others that feed the insecure ego's need to be knowledgeable, good, or right. Discovering and learning to accept these lost parts helps us actualize more of our unique human potential. As we embrace and welcome these parts, we become more whole.

Trauma and Trigger Reactions: Some Definitions

Psychologists and other mental health professionals have created a fairly refined set of labels and definitions for different types of nervous-system dysfunction. They use the term *shock trauma* for events that are sudden and overwhelming to the person's ability to cope. Examples of this would be witnessing a violent act or being in a tragic accident. These things can occur at any age. Experts use the term *developmental trauma* for neglectful, abusive, or chaotic situations that occur while a child is developing into adulthood, usually in one's family of origin. Developmental trauma generally occurs over time. It is not caused by a one-time event.

Generally, the word *trauma* refers to an event or series of events that overwhelm a person's ability to cope — whether this is a tragic car accident or parental neglect. This same word can also refer to the *effect* of a traumatic event, as in "She suffered a head *trauma*," or "She suffered an emotional *trauma*." A trauma is something that has happened in the past. It is generally believed that the effects of trauma are more lasting and severe if the traumatized person does not have an opportunity to process the event, talk about the event, or be comforted by someone else right after the event.

The word *trigger* means a current-time cue or event that restimulates the sensations of a past trauma. *Trigger* can be both a verb and a noun. A loud voice can *trigger* (verb) a person's fear of being controlled or overpowered. And this same loud voice is a *trigger* (noun) for the person to assume a self-protective posture. The original trauma behind this trigger might be early childhood experiences of being yelled at by a parent or the experience of being bullied at school by someone with a loud, scary voice. This book focuses mostly on people's *trigger reactions*, which are also sometimes called *trauma reactions*, and these generally involve some version of fight, flight, or freeze. In this case, if a loud voice was the trigger, the person might react by yelling back (fight), leaving the room (flight), or shutting down and not responding at all (freeze). Reactions can range from mild, like having a judgmental thought, to severe, like going numb. A triggering stimulus can sometimes cause a *flashback*. A flashback is a brief, vivid, often frightening memory that seems to appear out of nowhere and that makes people feel as if they are back in the traumatic situation. Sometimes flashbacks occur without any apparent stimulus.

Attachment Trauma

An important type of developmental trauma is called *attachment trauma*. This term refers to those all-too-common forms of neglect, abuse, or disorganized behavior that interfere with an infant or child's secure attachment or bonding with their caregiver. This disrupts a child's sense of trust that their needs matter or that it is safe to express their feelings and needs. Most people suffer some degree of attachment trauma simply because many parents are often too busy or too distracted with their own problems to be fully present to their child's needs. All children have attachment needs like loving attention, nurturing touch, and reassurances of safety when they are hurt or afraid. Such reassurance of safety by another human is called *coregulation*.

The need for parent-to-child coregulation continues beyond infancy, through one's childhood, and even into one's teens. Another attachment need that continues into one's teens is the need to have one's sovereignty or unique personhood respected. If a parent treats a child as an instrument to fulfill the parent's selfish needs, pleasure, or status, this is a violation of the child's sovereignty and can create wounding or insecure functioning.

The basic attachment need that seems to endure throughout life is the need to feel that we are not all alone, that there is someone we can turn to for comfort or reassurance in times of distress. Research shows that if a child or adult suffers a traumatic incident, but then has someone supportive to talk with about it, the effects of this trauma are much less severe.

Humans Are Not Machines

When people get triggered, they often say, "That person pushed my buttons." This phrase illustrates how a perceived threat to one's emotional safety can cause a person to go on automatic — just as if someone pushed a button on a machine. The button gets pushed, or the trigger pulled, and suddenly the person exhibits a series of a preprogrammed reactions or automated routines. Humans are not machines, but we often behave in machinelike ways — automatically explaining ourselves if someone says they do not agree with us, or automatically assuming our housemate is angry if we hear the door slam. My aim in writing this book is to show that we can overcome this unfortunate programming and open up to our full range of options and choices in any given moment — instead of being stuck in rigid, machinelike patterns.

The journey to mastering your triggers begins when you recognize reactivity in yourself. This reactivity can be obvious — like when you yell at the person who took your parking space. Or it can be hidden — like when someone interrupts you, and you feel slighted, but you don't want to make a big deal out of it. In this book, recognizing and working with your trigger reactions is the focus of part 1. The chapters are organized around five essential adult development tasks. These are the Five Steps of Trigger Work: admitting to and accepting triggers, catching them early, pausing to self-calm, activating self-compassion, and restoring safety and connection. These chapters provide simple practices for accomplishing each step, and they can be done by yourself.

Part 2 shows how to apply these practices in different types of relationships: with your mate, your children, a friend, as a group member, as a group leader, and in relationship to your social context.

Part One

Practices for
Transforming Reactivity

Chapter One

Getting from Here to There

The Five Steps of Trigger Work

As we do this work, we learn that having a hair-trigger reaction does not mean there is something shamefully wrong with us. We may come to feel some underlying sadness or grief that our childhood conditioning has set us up to experience such insecurities, but grief about such things is actually healthy.

Most people don't like to admit it when they get triggered. This normal, and quite understandable, aversion to emotional discomfort is the primary impediment to healing childhood wounds and showing up more present in daily life. This chapter overviews the five developmental tasks or life skills that constitute this healing journey, and the rest of the chapters in part 1 describe in detail how to accomplish each step. Here are the Five Steps of Trigger Work:

1. Admitting and accepting your insecurities
2. Learning your unique trigger signature
3. Pausing to regulate yourself
4. Being with sensations and emotions
5. Repairing and clearing the air

1. Admitting and Accepting Your Insecurities

Acceptance is achieved when you are able to notice and accept that you sometimes get triggered, that other people also get triggered, and that sometimes others get triggered by things that you do or say. You accept that a certain amount of emotional discomfort comes with the territory of relating with others. Acceptance also means you do not judge yourself as bad or wrong for getting triggered or for triggering someone else. You know it is normal. You may not like that you get triggered, but you know that it happens to almost everyone. Acceptance generally comes more easily to people whose trigger reactions are not too debilitating. If reactions are criticized by others or cause painful breakups or disruptions of friendships, then people may carry shame about the fact that they sometimes "lose it." If watching yourself get triggered seems unbearably painful, you may have to go slowly with some of the practices in this book. Going slowly is generally better than going too fast, anyway. It allows for deeper self-experiencing.

The inner work of the admitting and accepting stage involves coming to terms with insecure brain wiring, childhood trauma, shame, or all of the above. As we do this work, we learn that having a hair-trigger reaction does not mean there is something shamefully wrong with us. We may come to feel some underlying sadness or grief that our childhood conditioning has set us up to experience such insecurities, but grief about such things is actually healthy. It is part of the work of coming to terms with what happened. Grief helps us accept the facts of our early history. Eventually, we will no longer blame others for our reactions or spend much time wishing things were different.

Acceptance comes when we rise above the need to blame ourselves or someone else for our trigger reactions and sensitivities. "Rising above" means we can witness ourselves, the other person, and the whole context with some measure of objectivity. This takes practice. Doing the practices in this book will get you there.

At first, you might be unaware of when you are getting triggered — especially if your reactivity happens mostly on the inside and is not visible to others. Inside or invisible trigger reactions are things like having judgmental thoughts about the other, making assumptions about the other's motives, going blank, or being afraid to speak up. As you do the exercises in this book, you will grow in your ability to admit and accept that you sometimes get triggered.

2. Learning Your Unique Trigger Signature

Your handwriting has a characteristic look and feel. It may be small and constricted, big and bold, or somewhere in between. Similarly, most of your trigger reactions will look somewhat similar to one another and will arise from the same *core fear* (like fear of rejection, abandonment, not being good enough, not being heard, and so on). Our trigger signature is an expression of our attachment style. If we have a *preoccupied/anxious attachment style*, we are more likely to pursue, prod, question, argue, challenge, or attack when we get triggered. If we have a more *avoidant attachment style*, we tend to shut down, withdraw, defend, explain, judge silently, or try to fix things when we are triggered. Knowing your unique trigger signature helps you quickly recognize the fact that you are getting triggered. This is a big step toward trigger mastery.

However, I want to clarify that when I use labels like *preoccupied* or *avoidant*, my intent is to provide a potentially useful lens through which to view behavior patterns. Just as there are no pure types, no one is purely *avoidant*, purely *preoccupied*, or even purely *secure* in their attachment style. All behavior patterns fall somewhere along a continuum. So, for example, someone's behavior may demonstrate a *somewhat* avoidant style or a *somewhat* secure style. As you read, please remember that types and styles are not absolutes but describe tendencies.

Some more avoidant types will have difficulty noticing their trigger sensitivities because they only get triggered when someone else is upset with them. They may think they are the victim of someone else's triggers, as in: "If he didn't get triggered, I would be fine." For these people, their core fears or unconscious insecurities may be deeply buried, so that it takes an "explosion" (like a highly reactive or frustrating partner) to unearth their hidden fears. Maybe the developmental trauma/neglect that they experienced occurred before they had language or before they started to remember things. Children who were mildly neglected often develop into very resourceful, self-reliant little people who do not expect much from others. They may also have rather adaptable or pleasing personalities. This protects them so they don't feel as much disappointment or frustration as might otherwise be the case. Their dependency needs tend to be repressed, so they may not recognize the unmet needs underneath their buoyant or even-tempered personality structures. Thus, they could go through life never recognizing when their needs aren't being met — because they got used to not expecting much from others a long time ago.

By the time you begin to recognize what your trigger reactions look like and feel like, you already have some ability to notice and take ownership of the fact that you sometimes get triggered. That's part of the admitting and accepting step. But *noticing* a trigger reaction while in the midst of being reactive is not easy! When you are triggered, your ability to notice tends to go offline. That's why you need to practice pausing. This is the next step.

3. Pausing to Regulate Yourself

Pausing requires that you notice yourself doing some aspect of your trigger signature (like arguing or defending yourself), and you stop doing that. You can say "pause" to yourself or out loud. Some partners make a pause agreement, so that when either person says "pause," both will stop talking and silently take ten slow conscious breaths through the nose.

Self-regulation involves turning your attention inward and calming your nervous system, perhaps doing slow, deep breathing or some other body-awareness practice. This step is your first aid for reactivity. It is one of life's basic stress-management tools. I wish more grade schools would teach this, but it's never too late to learn. The challenge, of course, is learning to do this under one of life's most stressful conditions — being triggered by someone who is important to us.

4. Being with Sensations and Emotions

Once you have learned to consciously attend to your breath and body, you will find it easier to notice your sensations and emotions — the tension in your throat, the pain in your heart, any sadness, fear, or helplessness. This step involves taking the position of the "witness" or "noticer" — noticing the breath going in and out; noticing feelings, sensations, images, memories, and mind chatter; watching these internal impressions enter and exit your awareness field; watching for changes in their quality or intensity; watching them move around to different locations in your body. As the noticer, your attention is on the sensations being witnessed — so you are both *the one having sensations or feelings* and *the one witnessing yourself having sensations or feelings*. It's as if your awareness has two perspectives simultaneously. This enables you to hold space for yourself, to comfort yourself. This dual awareness is also the foundation for a more intimate or friendly relationship with yourself. When you learn how to be with yourself, you never have to feel all alone.

5. Repairing and Clearing the Air

If a trigger reaction (even a subtle reaction like withdrawing or freezing) occurs during an interaction with another person, it can be helpful to approach this person later to reconnect, repair the damages, apologize, or have a do-over. This step is not appropriate for some situations because it generally requires the other person's agreement or consent. So sometimes you will not use this step.

If the triggered behavior occurs with a partner or spouse, a close friend, or a child, then a repair will be necessary. In other situations, what is done for repair depends on the relationship — how close or interdependent people are, and how important the relationship is.

Typically, this step involves setting aside an agreed-upon time for repair, and then, once that time arrives, you will (1) acknowledge you were triggered; (2) apologize, if appropriate; (3) reveal the emotional roots of the reaction; and (4) ask for connection or reassurance. Repair looks something like this: "When I walked out, I was triggered. I'm sorry I did that. It was probably my fear coming up that my needs don't matter. If I could do it over, if I could tell you what was really in my heart, I wish I could have asked for reassurance that we're okay and that my needs do matter."

These five steps, while they each involve their own specific practices, are also interdependent — so a gain in one of the five areas will result in a gain in all areas. For example, the better you get at offering compassion to yourself, the easier it will be to accept that you get triggered. Or the sooner you are able to execute a pause, the easier the repair step will go, since you stop yourself from saying hurtful things and will have less "damage" to repair. Even though these five steps are presented sequentially, they are actually mutually reinforcing.

Chapter Two

Admitting and Accepting Your Insecurities

Getting Beyond Shame and Blame

When triggering happens, no one is to blame. No one chooses to feel at the mercy of their own or another person's primitive brain wiring.

When you are triggered, you are not the best version of yourself. You may feel hurt, shocked, or out of control. You might appear foolish, impulsive, defensive, or irrational. Your ability to cope is compromised — so it's no wonder you might have trouble accepting this when it happens. But as any therapist or change agent would say, we need to be where we are to get where we want to go. In other words, positive change requires fully owning, feeling, getting to know, and taking responsibility for where we are right now in our growth journey. If there are parts of ourselves that we are denying or repressing, these parts won't heal until we see and accept them. They won't be able to find their rightful relationship with the healthier aspects of our being because there is no communication between these different parts of ourselves. The hallmark of a healthy system (such as a person, group, or organization) is good communication between the subparts of that system.

Some people have an easier time than others accepting the fact that they get triggered. You will discover your own personal degree of resistance versus acceptance as you work through the exercises in this book. If your self-image can accommodate making mistakes, making amends, looking foolish or inept in the eyes of others, and not always knowing the right thing to do, then you will probably have an easier time accepting your trigger reactions. If your self-image has little tolerance for mistakes, weaknesses, or imperfections, you'll probably find it harder to accept that you get triggered. But in any case, the insecurities that give rise to self-judgment and perfectionism can be healed.

Whether you place more value on *learning from mistakes* versus *needing to be right and looking good* depends a lot on what felt safe versus unsafe as you were growing up, as your personality was being formed. Your value stance (learning versus looking good) will gradually change as you work through the exercises in this book. When you make learning your primary value, life gets a lot easier ... and friendlier.

These exercises will also help you learn to recognize the subtle signs that indicate you and others are triggered. People do not always get loud or argumentative when they are triggered. Reactivity is often mostly internal — like having suspicious or judgmental thoughts.

Trigger reactions arise from feeling emotionally unsafe or unable to cope. We unconsciously associate what is happening now with something that happened a long time ago — something that felt unsafe or overwhelming — with respect to our core developmental needs, like the need to feel valued, respected, protected, cared for, attended to, and important. Then we react with some version of upset, ranging from exploding to shutting down to projecting negative motives onto others (such as, "He's using me," "She's controlling me," and so on). All of these reactions can occur below the level of conscious awareness. People can feel unsafe without being aware of it.

If you are already aware that sometimes you do not feel safe or capable, then you are well on your way to accepting that you sometimes get triggered. Obviously, it's better to feel safe than unsafe, and it helps to have personal practices to quickly restore your sense of emotional safety after any upsetting event. When we feel safe, we can see more of what's really going on. We make decisions based on our authentic needs, like the need to feel respected or trusted, rather than on conditioned habits like defensiveness or self-protection. This is the ultimate goal of all this inner work: making good decisions that come from the higher brain versus the primitive lizard brain. Let's start this journey toward good decision-making by taking an honest, compassionate look at our insecurities.

Admitting Insecurities

Even though the concept of being triggered is now widely recognized, most people still have difficulty accepting that, when they themselves get triggered, their upset feelings arise from their own inner world. But trigger sensitivities reveal useful information. If someone says something that triggers our own insecurity or pain, this pain or fear was already in us waiting to be activated. When we get triggered, it signals there is something incomplete in our development or some aspect of us that is being denied, repressed, rejected, or disowned. In other words, even though we did not cause the triggering event, it is ours to deal with every time it appears. It is our own responsibility to find a way to restore a sense of safety and equilibrium to our dysregulated nervous system. Intellectual acceptance of this idea is not so hard. But when we find ourselves behaving in a way we're not proud of, shame can come up ... or the impulse to blame.

Acceptance requires admitting our insecurities — because it is mainly our childhood insecurities that make us vulnerable to emotional dysregulation, to those fight, flight, or freeze reactions that most of us are familiar with. Childhood insecurities may include things like fears of not being enough or of being flawed, unimportant, insignificant, unworthy, helpless, alone, disrespected, overwhelmed, trapped, controlled, unloved, or unlovable. Insecurities are *fears* about what might be true. Harboring fears like these does not mean that we actually are flawed, unimportant, and so on. Triggers are based on fears, not actualities. Depending on how much inner work you have already done, you may find it easy or difficult to notice and acknowledge these sorts of fears.

Most of these fears got installed in our personality as we were growing up. Even with the best of parents, children often "learn the wrong thing" about themselves. Children tend to take things personally, so when they aren't able to get what they want, they naively conclude that something is wrong with themselves. If no one comes to feed a crying infant, that infant may subconsciously conclude that they are unimportant, not valued, not worthy, or unlovable.

When we are small children surrounded by, and somewhat

dependent on, adults, it is almost guaranteed that we will occasionally fall short in our efforts to cope with life's challenges or get our needs met. We are little and dependent — it's normal to feel bewildered or helpless at times. This can trigger those "not good enough" feelings that so many adults carry deep inside. One might even conclude that feeling insecure is part of the human condition. There is a "maybe I'm not enough" part of everyone. Getting triggered helps us locate this part and do what is needed to heal our early wounding and faulty learning.

The bottom line is: Almost everyone gets triggered, some more than others, and some more noticeably than others. Getting triggered more frequently or less frequently does not make someone worse or better than anyone else. But sometimes, when we see ourselves getting triggered, this will reinforce the belief that we are flawed or not good enough. The self-healing program in this book will teach you to bring compassion to the parts of you that were frustrated, hurt, or traumatized as a little person. Self-compassion is something you can learn. It is an antidote for shame.

What Brain Science Has to Offer

Many scientific insights have emerged over the past forty years that help us understand the biological basis of how triggering happens. Understanding the neuropsychology of triggers can help us accept that, under a perceived threat, humans are neurologically wired to shoot first and ask questions later, to react first and then investigate. This does not justify harmful behavior that results from being triggered, but it helps to understand that the instinctual part of our brain is truly a powerful force to be reckoned with. To one degree or another, we are all at the mercy of our biological instincts, which is why being triggered does not make someone bad, wrong, weak, or crazy. Further, understanding how the brain works helps us be more realistic about what can and cannot be controlled by good intentions, positive thinking, or better communication skills. You can learn to halt and heal reactive behavior patterns, but this takes engaging somatically with the practices described here.

I believe that too many teachers and authors, as well as regular people, do not fully take into account the power of a triggered nervous system. We can be easily seduced by the lure of the cognitive quick fix — like the idea "don't take anything personally" (as if it were that easy!), or the idea to replace an old negative belief by repeating a new positive one. Once we understand the inner workings of our brain, and how to work somatically, mindfully, and compassionately with our reactive mind, we can gain more conscious control. We can learn to have more voluntary control of our involuntary trigger reactions.

But we need to start by recognizing what a powerful force we are dealing with. Since your trigger reactions arise from aspects of yourself that are largely unconscious, stop thinking that you or other people *should* have better self-control or *should* behave more rationally. No one decides to get triggered, nor do they intend to trigger their intimate partner or their adult offspring. When I hear someone say, "He likes to push my buttons," I believe this is generally not true. This is a "reactive story" that helps that person avoid their own deeper feelings and needs about the situation. Of course, a person with a narcissistic or sociopathic personality disorder will intentionally push buttons as a manipulation, but this is usually not what's going on. When someone's behavior triggers our core fears or insecurities, this fear was usually already hiding in the shadows of our personality structure. It probably originated in some earlier experience of neglect, trauma, abuse, or faulty learning. The person who has just triggered us did not cause our sensitivity to feeling hurt or slighted in this way. That sensitivity was already there — as a result of unfortunate early learning experiences that occurred long before we met this person.

Brain science explains reactivity in terms of how the brain is wired. The human brain has a lot in common with the brains of other animals. Our brains are equipped with what neuropsychologists call the *survival alarm system*. Part of this system is a tiny pair of structures deep inside the midbrain called the *amygdalae*, or the *amygdala* in common parlance. This set of structures has a primary role in the processing of emotions like fear, anxiety, or anger/aggression. Like radar, our survival alarm is always scanning for danger. As with other animals, this alarm system was built into the human species to quickly accelerate our bodies into action if a predatory animal was even suspected to be nearby. Whenever a potential threat is detected, neurons in this area fire loudly, like an alarm. Today, for humans, this threat is more often associated with a disturbance in our connection to others or in our sense of efficacy to get our needs met. The things that threaten us nowadays are primarily interpersonal.

When our survival alarm is ringing, strong neurochemicals (like adrenaline and cortisol) are sent to various parts of the autonomic nervous system, causing certain bodily systems to go into action — like heart rate and limb strength — because this helps us mobilize for aggression or for running away. Our survival alarm chemicals signal other systems to shut down — like digestion and sex — because these are less vital to immediate survival. Brain scientists remind us that when we don't feel like eating or we have no interest in sex, this may be related to feeling unsafe, anxious, or threatened. Maybe there's an unprocessed trigger reaction somewhere in our psyche that needs attention. Maybe our survival alarm is stuck in the On position. Remember, all of these neurochemical reactions are below the level of conscious awareness. We do not choose any of this. But if we can accept that trigger reactions are due to the workings of the survival alarm system — which has become especially sensitized to threats in human connection similar to those that happened in childhood — then we are well on our way to accepting our trigger reactions.

In addition, current research shows that things like a sharp voice tone or a disapproving facial expression can trigger an automatic impulse to attack, defend, or run away, as if a tiger has suddenly appeared. Even in the absence of any threat to our physical survival, our inner alarms warn about threats to our emotional safety and security and to our social connections and intimate relationships.

Have you ever gotten triggered by someone's voice tone? Some women feel unsafe hearing a loud, booming male voice. I, personally, sometimes feel something akin to the fear of being dominated or overpowered. Some men have a similar reaction to a shrill or harsh female voice. My men friends tell me that this sometimes triggers them to think they are being criticized or disapproved of. Many people tell me that they often try to overlook such inner reactions and go on conversing as if nothing had triggered them. For mild triggers, this may work fine. But I think it's more beneficial in the long run to recognize when our conversations have been taken over by the primitive part of our brain. Both people could be communicating while on autopilot and not even know it.

For instance, brain research has shown that when two or more people feel emotionally connected or interdependent, they become "wired together," meaning that if one person gets triggered, the others closest to them usually become triggered as well. This cotriggering is normal, and yet it happens below the level of conscious awareness. This makes it difficult to know who got triggered first, which in the end doesn't really matter. What's important to remember is that if your partner gets triggered, your nervous system may feel unsafe and get cotriggered, so you both will need to pause, become aware of this, and practice self-calming.

Obviously, people are not at their best when their survival alarm is triggered. The quick, knee-jerk reactions like fight, flight, or freeze cause people to yell, blow up, blame, try to be right, distance, shut down, avoid, build walls, get silent, or become defensive. And afterward, they often do not recall what they actually did or said or even what triggered them. Sometimes people think they're ready to talk it out and resolve things with the other person, but it can be too soon. They're not feeling calm and safe enough yet. They may still be in a self-protective mode. Trying to resolve things when they feel that way can make things worse.

Sometimes it takes quite a while to feel calm and safe again. At high levels of activation, the survival alarm can dramatically hijack the higher brain. Remember, this alarm system is the part of the brain that primitive humans depended on for their actual physical survival. Our higher brain functions go offline because they operate too slowly to save us from a saber-toothed tiger! When our survival alarm is ringing, everything feels like an emergency, so we have to really work to get calm again. Only when our survival alarm is turned off, and we are feeling safe with the other person, will our higher brain functions be available enough to resolve the issue or repair the misunderstanding. Only then can we feel empathy and understanding for the other person's needs and be able to communicate our own vulnerable feelings — like the wish to feel loved and connected. As long as we don't feel safe, our mind is not spacious enough to deeply listen to the other person. If we try to repair too soon, without doing some inner self-calming and self-soothing, we'll probably just retrigger one another and be back where we started. For more on how to know if you are trying to repair too soon, see chapter 6.

Acceptance Comes Little by Little

As this short review of brain science shows, triggering is part of the human condition. When triggering happens, no one is to blame. No one chooses to feel at the mercy of their own or another person's primitive brain wiring. But it happens. This is why, when triggering episodes happen, we should first acknowledge and accept them rather than berate ourselves. Acceptance gets easier as we practice the self-calming, self-compassion, and repair techniques in chapters 4, 5, and 6. Once we learn how to recover quickly from reactivity, it becomes easier to accept such reactions and sensitivities. In my experience, the work of acceptance is not complete until these additional practices have become integrated into our lives — as something we do every time there is a triggering episode.

In fact, to get better at this, I recommend practicing the self-calming and self-compassion exercises in chapters 4 and 5 at times when you're not actively triggered. When you feel strong and confident, voluntarily bring back the memory of an event when you were triggered. Remember how you felt, and then practice self-calming and self-compassion. The aim is to get so familiar with your reactions and core fears that, eventually, when triggering happens, you'll be able to say to yourself: *Ah, here it is again. I know this place. I'm triggered, and I know what to do. I know how to get calm and "be with" my tender or upset part. I know that this pain passes quickly when I do that.*

Your Beliefs About Triggers: A Self-Assessment Quiz

Before reading further, I suggest taking this self-assessment quiz in order to become more aware of your current beliefs and attitudes related to triggering. There are some commonly held false assumptions and unrealistic beliefs that many people hold without realizing it, and these can make acceptance of being triggered more difficult. After you answer the following ten questions, add up your total score. Then I discuss what various scores may indicate about someone's level of acceptance and offer advice about how to be more accepting of triggers.

For each question, either on a separate piece of paper or in the book, write a number between 1 and 4: 1 means you strongly disagree with this statement or it is never true of you; 2 means you slightly agree with the statement or it is sometimes true of you; 3 means you mostly agree with this statement or it is frequently true of you; and 4 means you strongly agree with the statement or it is always true for you.

1. If my partner gets upset by an innocent remark from me, I believe I should stop saying this sort of thing.

2. After an upsetting interaction, when I later realize that I have taken someone's words personally and overreacted, I spend a lot of time going over it in my mind, trying to justify why I reacted that way.

3. If incidents of emotional reactivity happen more than a few times a week with me and my partner, I judge this to be a dysfunctional relationship.

4. If I am receiving unfavorable feedback from someone about my behavior, and I get triggered hearing it, I try to hide this. The other person could get the impression that I am fragile or thin-skinned.

5. To admit that I sometimes get triggered by my kids or by children is very difficult for me. I think this shows that I am immature or self-centered.

6. In an interaction where both people are triggered at once, it's useful to figure out who got triggered first.

7. If I have told someone over and over that a certain behavior is upsetting to me, I expect the person to stop doing that behavior.

8. After I have gotten triggered by someone's behavior, and they later apologize to me, I don't get any real comfort from their verbal apology. Talk is cheap. If they are really sorry, I expect a change in their behavior in the future.

9. If my intimate partner keeps blaming me for causing their trigger reactions, I try to get them to recognize that each of us is responsible for our own reactions.

10. When someone tells me they got triggered by something I did, I tend to assume I did something wrong, even if logic tells me otherwise.

To find your total score, add up the numbers you wrote next to each item. A score of 10 to 12 means you have a pretty realistic and accepting attitude toward emotional triggers. A score of 13 to 20 means you are probably ambivalent about triggering and are sometimes uncertain what to do when it happens. A score above 20 indicates that you struggle with triggers; you tend to deny, resist, and have trouble coping with being triggered. I discuss the reasons for these difficulties below, but here are the most common: Some people have little life experience or skills to deal with triggers; some have a tendency toward black-and-white thinking, with little tolerance for ambiguity; and some are not very accepting of their own and others' foibles. Finally, if someone is currently in a painful relationship that is causing much distress, it can be hard to be objective. A high score can also indicate that someone was triggered while taking the quiz.

Exploring Your Answers

Now let's look at each individual item in the quiz to explore what various answers reveal about someone's beliefs about triggers.

1. If my partner gets upset by an innocent remark from me, I believe I should stop saying this sort of thing.

In my experience, people who do not agree with this statement (that is, rate this a 1 or 2) have a pretty realistic attitude toward triggers. Rating this higher (with a 3 or 4) may indicate the belief that triggers always need to be avoided. This belief may cause a person to put too much of their attention on trying not to upset anyone — so they walk on eggshells. The fact is, people can be triggered by any unintended remark, and there is not much anyone can do to anticipate this. Your partner may have very different sensitivities than you do. Yes, you can and should learn to speak from your own experience and learn your partner's love language (and their fear language!), but no matter how good your communication skills, triggering may still happen.

Instead of walking on eggshells to avoid ever saying anything that might trigger someone, it's better to accept that people carry emotional baggage that others aren't aware of, and even innocent, well-intentioned remarks can be taken wrong. Better to accept that triggering will happen, and when it does, learn how to pause sooner and repair quicker (as later chapters describe). Then triggering itself will become less of a big deal.

2. After an upsetting interaction, when I later realize that I have taken someone's words personally and overreacted, I spend a lot of time going over it in my mind, trying to justify why I reacted that way.

If you gave this question a high rating (a 3 or 4), I hope this book will help you accept that we all sometimes overreact, and when we do, it's normal to feel foolish, embarrassed, exposed, or even ashamed. These feelings need not be a problem — once we learn to attend to and "hold" these feelings with a gentle, forgiving attitude. When we allow ourselves to have these feelings, this is an act of self-acceptance. Allowing uncomfortable feelings, while attending to them with a compassionate witnessing presence, makes room for change. This gives formerly contracted energies the space to breathe — to dissipate, relax, or find resolution (for more on this, see "Compassionate Self-Inquiry," pages 97–103).

When people can't accept the fact that they overreacted, they tend to obsess about the incident and try to find something or someone to blame for why they are upset. They might blame themselves, their partner, or the fact that they were tired or hungry. They might blame their childhood. Trying to figure it out gives people a sense of control, but these attempts often prevent deeper healing. They can keep us from getting to the root of the problem — which requires a more somatic and heart-centered relationship to our emotions.

To get to acceptance, the first step is to notice when your mind is going around and around about an incident — perhaps going over what the other person should or should not have done, or perhaps trying to justify why you have good reason to be upset. When you notice this sort of rumination or feel the need to defend your actions, this is a good entry point for inner work. See if you can be open and curious about where your hurt or angry feelings are coming from. Inner work means sitting with your reactive feelings — sort of like a therapist sits with a client or like a mother holds a hurting child. A good mother or therapist does not validate someone's defenses, they validate their tender, vulnerable feelings — helping them learn to make space for and empathize with these feelings (see chapter 5 for more on this).

3. If incidents of emotional reactivity happen more than a few times a week with me and my partner, I judge this to be a dysfunctional relationship.

People who give this statement a high rating (a 3 or 4) tend to have little tolerance for emotional discomfort. Each of us has our own unique capacity to cope with emotional pain without becoming overwhelmed. There is no absolute *good* or *normal*. Some people, due to their particular life experiences, have come to expect a fair amount of upset, anger, conflict, and even violence. Others become quite destabilized after seemingly minor upsets. I have known people who take a week or two to recover after getting a negative performance review at work. If you agreed with this item, you may possess a level of emotional sensitivity that needs to be honored. Genetics play a role here, too. Early childhood research has shown that some babies are born with more sensitive nervous systems — they are more sensitive to loud noises, to the sensation of being dropped, and so on.

If you are regularly triggered by someone, whether they are a romantic or work partner, that doesn't mean the relationship is necessarily dysfunctional. It may mean the other person is more thick-skinned, or perhaps you just cannot stand it when anyone is unhappy with you — even the slightest bit unhappy. If so, practice the trigger work in this book to see if things improve before giving up on a relationship.

That said, I believe a sensitive person needs to take care not to get into situations that repeatedly overwhelm their nervous system. If trigger reactivity is regular and extreme, and if partners can't create a sense of mutual safety together, I recommend getting personal or relationship counseling with someone trained in this type of trigger work.

4. If I am receiving unfavorable feedback from someone about my behavior, and I get triggered hearing it, I try to hide this. The other person could get the impression that I am fragile or thin-skinned.

A person's rating of this statement tends to reflect their level of concern about projecting a competent image. There is nothing wrong with being concerned about one's self-image; this is good to admit. But if you gave this a high rating (a 3 or 4), it can be useful to explore what you are trying to avoid. If you openly admit getting triggered, what negative consequences do you fear? When considering this question, does a particular individual come to mind — someone you really want to look good for? If so, reflect on how you feel in this person's presence, and consider if they remind you of any other important person from an earlier stage in your life. When you were younger, did you receive criticism for showing weakness, being too sensitive, or not being perfect?

No matter how you rated this question, try this stretch exercise: Bring to mind a memory of a time you got triggered by someone's words or actions and did not reveal this. Now ask yourself what you were afraid would happen if you revealed your reaction. Next, imagine revealing your reaction to the person who triggered you. What does it feel like to say these words inside your own head? Do you feel a sense of relief, lightness, inner power? Or is it more like tentativeness, apology, shame? Do words come easily, or do you have trouble coming up with what to say? Ultimately, just see what you discover during this exercise, and be compassionate toward yourself for any fear that may arise.

This type of inner inquiry helps us to know ourselves better, and it reflects the premise that informs this book: I believe that every unpleasant thing that occurs, whether inside us or in the world, can be the starting point for knowing ourselves in a deeper way. Further, I believe it is helpful, whenever we notice fear arising, to pause in the midst of our normal activities and to inquire into the roots of this fear. Chapter 5 has more practices for inner inquiry.

5. To admit that I sometimes get triggered by my kids or by children is very difficult for me. I think this shows that I am immature or self-centered.

People who agree with this statement (rating it a 3 or 4) view getting triggered by a child as something that should not happen, or at least should not happen to them. They fear how their kids or their intimate partner might view them. Or they might be reminded of a parent who actually is or was self-centered or immature, and they fear acting like this person, whom they do not want to be like.

However you rated this question, read it again very slowly, and as you read, notice if any feelings, sensations, images, or memories arise in you. If you discover any emotional charge or body contraction, let your attention rest there for a bit. Bring some openhearted curiosity to the matter — as if whatever you discover or don't discover will be okay with you. Simply look around in that corner of your inner world. Maybe you won't see anything very interesting or noteworthy. Or maybe a forgotten memory will surface — perhaps of an adult expressing upset emotions to a child in a way that scares the child. If that child in your memory is *you*, see if you can feel empathy for yourself as a child. Feeling empathy for a tender or hurting part of ourselves is an act of self-healing.

While doing these exercises, if recalling unhappy memories ever becomes too upsetting, bring yourself back into the present by doing one of the conscious breathing or grounding exercises in chapter 4.

6. In an interaction where both people are triggered at once, it's useful to figure out who got triggered first.

Ultimately, people who give this a low rating (a 1 or 2) tend to recognize that identifying who "started" a cotriggering incident is not the most important concern. However, when done for the right reasons, I believe there is nothing wrong with attempting to discover the origin or the larger context of a cotriggering incident. Just know that the real origin may be complex and go back a very long way.

For some people who agree with this statement (rate it 3 or 4), the main reason they want to unravel who got triggered first is to show that they didn't "start it." They believe they will feel better about themselves if it's the other person's fault. But this rarely helps or leads to truly feeling better. Fault-finding is often used to avoid experiencing one's real feelings.

Sometimes, examining the whole context of what happened prior to a cotriggering incident can be useful, though it may involve going back in time quite a long way. Any important relationship has a history of unrepaired ruptures that are going to affect our present-time interactions to some degree. So it may be useful to acknowledge that these people have shared a lot of experiences where one or both parties ended up feeling unfinished, unsafe, or unsatisfied. A backlog of these unrepaired ruptures can lead both parties to be more triggerable as time goes by. This is why it is difficult to know who or what started a current incident.

For any single unfinished situation, each person will probably feel "unfinished" about different aspects of that shared experience, and those feelings can trigger later reactions. For instance, if one person does something hurtful and later apologizes, the other person may not feel satisfied with that apology.

They may create a story in their mind that the other person didn't sound sincere or something like that. Meanwhile, the person who apologized might feel they never got acknowledged for trying to make amends, and think, *Nothing I do is ever enough.* Then, days or months later, when each person gets triggered by the other, it may be the result of a backlog of unfortunate fear-stories like these that have not been examined and repaired.

7. If I have told someone over and over that a certain behavior is upsetting to me, I expect the person to stop doing that behavior.

People who give this statement a high rating (a 3 or 4) tend to not understand or fully appreciate how hard it is to change triggered behavior. Generally, real, lasting change takes work on the part of both people. Of course, asking for what you want, in specific, noncomplaining language, is a good thing. But expecting to always get what you want is unwise. The other person may wish to grant your request, but sometimes they are not in full conscious control of their actions.

People have voluntary control over many of their actions, but some behaviors and reactions are the product of habit, personality type, childhood conditioning, or trigger reactions. Although we all want to be able to choose our responses in all instances, we will perhaps never be completely free from past conditioning.

In my couple counseling sessions, people often express unrealistic expectations about this: A wife, Sally, will say to her husband, Rick, "When I'm upset with you, just validate my experience and offer empathy. Don't defend yourself." To Sally, this seems like a reasonable request. Indeed, Rick might agree that he should and will do this from now on, and he may sincerely try to follow through. But even with the best of intentions, Rick may fail more than he succeeds — because when Sally gets upset, Rick gets cotriggered. In his triggered state (even if he doesn't look triggered to Sally), he is incapable of validating and empathizing; all his good intentions get overpowered by the strong neurochemicals that are flooding in. When Rick's nervous system is in "flight" mode, his instinct is to reason with Sally in an attempt to get her to stop being upset.

If Rick is to have a real chance at changing his behavior, Sally has to accept that she can't expect Rick to do all the work on his own. If Rick is going to learn to pause or slow down when he catches himself getting defensive, he needs her help, understanding, and support. They are going to have to work together to create what therapists call a *corrective emotional experience*. If Rick asks for a pause, instead of defending, and Sally requests reassurance, instead of criticizing, then this corrective emotional experience will help both of them feel safer.

8. After I have gotten triggered by someone's behavior, and they later apologize to me, I don't get any real comfort from their verbal apology. Talk is cheap. If they are really sorry, I expect a change in their behavior in the future.

This statement sounds similar to statement 7, and they have a lot in common, but this highlights a slightly different misunderstanding when it comes to triggers. People who rate this highly (with a 3 or 4) tend to be generally suspicious of apologies — possibly due to painful early experiences with someone who hurt them and then apologized repeatedly. Their understandable suspiciousness makes it very difficult for a current partner to repair a mistake. Partners are not perfect. They will sometimes do things that upset us. And if we cannot accept apologies, every triggering event is probably going to be more scary — both for us and for our partner. This can lead a partner to walk on eggshells in an effort to never trigger their partner. This isn't usually sustainable. And it's also not really healthy for one partner to adapt to the other's every need and sensitivity.

While there is nothing wrong with wishing a partner would stop doing the things that trigger us, it is better to own responsibility for getting triggered, so we can address coreactivity together in a way that is cooperative, rather than one-sided.

When working with triggers, I suggest adopting a "life is a practice" mindset. Become curious whenever you notice a strong resistance in yourself to someone's behavior. Try to recognize anything that you consistently judge or resist — or any way you try to get somebody else to change their behavior so as not to trigger you. What developmental need (such as feeling loved or feeling good enough) are you trying to get met? When you can name this need, this is the beginning of compassionate acceptance.

9. If my intimate partner keeps blaming me for causing their trigger reactions, I try to get them to recognize that each of us is responsible for our own reactions.

Most blaming statements are unhealthy, unhelpful, and probably untrue, and of course, no one likes to be blamed. But it's fair to ask: *If I am always trying to get my partner to stop blaming me, does this mean* fear of being blamed *is one of my triggers?* This might be true of you if you rated this item a 3 or 4. Some people become vigilant about protecting themselves from being seen as bad or wrong, and they see (or imagine) the intent to blame in every contentious interaction.

Further, blaming may be the other person's go-to reactive

behavior, their major defense mechanism. It's how the person protects themselves when they get triggered. If this is true in a relationship, the best, most realistic practice is to simply call for a pause every time blaming arises.

The pause agreement is very important, as it's necessary for taking the next steps of inner inquiry and repair (the process described in chapters 4, 5, and 6). These steps can serve to correct mistaken blaming stories. At first, the practices need to be followed with a certain degree of faith. A reactive behavior like blaming might continue, but over time the practices lead both people to a new place. These practices are designed to help everyone get beyond the tendency to blame by helping people value their own inner development over the need to feel blameless.

10. When someone tells me they got triggered by something I did, I tend to assume I did something wrong, even if logic tells me otherwise.

People who rate this statement high (with a 3 or 4) tend to believe that they *are* to blame for triggering others, along with believing that, by changing their behavior, they can avoid triggering someone. I think it is more helpful to assume that while we can help others overcome their reactive behavior through reassurance and repair, we cannot completely avoid triggering others, no matter how hard we try.

People who scored high on this statement may have grown up in a home where they learned to adapt to the family situation so as not to create waves. They may have had a parent or older sibling whose behavior was erratic, unpredictable, or unsafe. Maybe the best option, or the only safe option, was to adapt — to bend, mold, or hide their true needs in order to create more equilibrium in the family system. Good behavior kept the child or teen out of the line of fire, or it might have helped ease the parents' burden or stress. Children are dependent on their parents for survival, and so helping parents by adapting can be a smart thing to do. So being good and trying not to make waves became the person's primary personality strategy.

For some people, their family home was not so intense, but they still did not like upsetting others or doing anything that generated annoyance, disappointment, or disapproval. So to avoid those things, they adapted. Whatever the reason, these people may have focused too much attention growing up on how other people were doing, thus limiting their own authentic self-expression.

Adapting so as not to create discomfort or disapproval in others does not necessarily come from growing up in a dysfunctional family. Some develop this reaction due to negative peer experiences in school that fostered sensitivity to negative feedback in a group setting. I have seen this as a facilitator of highly interactive groups, where members are encouraged to give one another feedback on the impact of their behavior. In these sorts of groups, and also in business team meetings, it is very common for a person to get negative feedback from just one other person in the group, after which this person instantly makes up a rule that they should never do or say this thing again — the thing that only one person didn't like. I recall one group where someone was asked a question and responded, "I don't feel like answering that." Someone else then said to this person, "I thought that was harsh. Why didn't you want to answer?" The person looked at the floor and didn't reply, but a few minutes later announced: "I guess, in this group, we're supposed to answer every question someone asks."

When someone disapproves of us, it's common to assume we did something wrong. We must accept the fact that we will inadvertently trigger some people at times, and we may never fully understand why. By mastering the practices in this book, you will come to accept that all self-expression contains a risk that someone won't agree or approve, and you'll be able to bounce back quickly from reactivity, whether it's your own or other people's.

Resistance Is Normal

Even though the word *triggered* is now part of our vocabulary, most people still have difficulty accepting full ownership for the fact that when we get emotionally reactive, this arises from our own inner world. If someone else's words trigger feelings of insecurity or pain, this pain was already inside waiting to be activated. Even if we intellectually accept this, we may still have some emotional resistance.

Here are the three most common emotional blocks to such acceptance:

1. **Shame** — the belief that if I get triggered, this means I am flawed, that there is something deeply wrong with me.
2. **Mistrust** — the fear that if I own my reactions as "mine," and become more forgiving of the person whose behavior triggered me, this gives the other person a free pass, and they don't have to mend their ways.
3. **Protecting one's parents** — the need to view one's childhood as happy and the need to view one's parents as good.

Shame

The roots of shame could be childhood abuse or neglect, such as when a child thinks, *If this person could treat me like this, I must be worthless*. It could be a painful public failure experience, in which the child feels not good enough or ashamed because they did not do well. It could be the consistent childhood experience of being overcontrolled, so that the child assumes, *I am not allowed to have a sovereign self. I do not matter, I have no worth*. It could stem from having something horrible happen or from committing a horrible act (even accidentally). Whatever the source, shame makes us want to hide, to not be seen, even though we may have an equally strong need to be seen at other times. The antidote for shame is self-compassion — the ability to activate the innate healing power of our "good mother archetype," the part of the human unconscious that is instinctively nurturing and unconditionally loving. The exercise "Being with Sensations and Emotions" (page 20) will show you how to access your inner "good mother."

Mistrust

In working with couples, I sometimes hear one partner protesting, "Why should I be the one to change? Why should I have to be the grown-up? This will just make it easier for my partner to keep being immature and selfish. Or maybe my partner will use my admission of my insecurities as ammunition against me by telling me later how insecure I am." Usually, when a person says this type of thing, they are afraid of being hurt. They believe they have tried being "the grown-up" in the past, and this has not been appreciated or recognized by their partner. Or they believe they have tried being vulnerable, and this has come back to them later in the form of criticism.

So they are not willing to do any more inner work. They think it is their partner's turn to do his work.

Unfortunately, whatever happened in the past that gave rise to this person's fear-story (such as, "If I'm vulnerable, they'll use it against me") was probably a cotriggering event (or series of events) that never got repaired, and now it is almost impossible to know what actually happened. When relationship ruptures go unrepaired, partners store fear-based reactive stories about the partner in long-term memory, and such stories are very hard to dislodge. The interpretation of events occurred when higher brain capacities were offline, and there is no recording of what actually happened. Even if there was, the triggered brain was interpreting that event through the lens of unconscious fears, so objectivity was impossible. This sort of relationship mistrust can be healed by consistently doing the trigger-work practices in this book until both people realize that their mistrustful thoughts about the other are what I call a *reactive story* or a *fear-story*. Holding a reactive story like this is a sign that we are in a triggered state. It is wise to view such fear-stories as we would any other trigger reaction. If we can label such mistrustful thoughts as "fear-stories," they will have less power over us.

Protecting One's Parents

Many children learn to protect or take care of their parents during childhood. They try not to make too many demands. They deny their own needs and hurts. They make excuses for a parent's immature behavior. So as an adult, they continue this pattern of protecting the parent by overlooking or minimizing the parent's weaknesses or poor decisions and denying that they have any unresolved childhood wounds. The need for such denial has many origins, which often become apparent as we explore our trigger reactions. But this need to protect evaporates as we strengthen our capacity to tolerate and "be with" the emotional pain of our neglected, abused, or traumatized parts.

The pattern of protecting the good name of one's parents might also arise from the need to project a positive self-image, as a compensation for some imagined lack or flaw in oneself. So we might expand this positivity bias to include our entire childhood and family of origin.

When someone first starts looking into how well their childhood needs were met, they may truly believe that they do not get triggered and that their parents were ideal. But as exploration continues, they will probably recall ways that their parents disappointed them or weren't able to meet their needs. No parent can meet a child's every need, so some childhood frustration is a necessary part of a child's growth. Eventually, most people recall some of the pain, disappointment, or frustration they felt as a child. Feeling sadness when remembering childhood disappointment does not mean the person had bad parenting. And it does not mean the person is blaming the parents for their feelings of sadness. It's more about feeling empathy for this younger self or sorrow for some of the things they experienced as a child.

Accepting the facts of your life, including your early family life, is the first step in healing yourself.

The Payoff of Acceptance

Gaining deeper understanding regarding your own and others' trigger reactions allows you to adopt a worldview that sees everything that shows up in your life as acceptable and deal-with-able. You may not like a particular unwanted event, but here it is, so the question becomes: How do I feel about it, how can I be with this feeling in a self-loving way, and how shall I deal with it in a self-respecting way? When you feel resistance to an event, including some ordinary irritant like someone's voice tone, what inner fear or insecurity is at the root of this resistance? How current or realistic is this fear? If it is not current or realistic, your fear is probably some version of a trigger reaction. Once you accept it as a trigger reaction, now you're empowered to do something constructive (rather than remain stuck in resistance, reaction, or denial).

It is easier to accept your trigger reactions once you learn how to compassionately embrace any shame or resistance and move quickly from being triggered to being centered again. The exercises in part I show you what you can do once you accept your trigger reaction to restore your inner sense of calmness, confidence, worthiness, and safety.

There is always inner work to be done to get from *resisting what is* to *accepting what is*, and then to *getting into a new relationship with what is*. This is certainly the case with trigger reactions. This book shows you not only how to more easily accept that triggering happens inside of you, but also how to accept that other people in your world get triggered. That's an equally important part of the work of acceptance.

Acceptance helps you focus your efforts and attention on the parts of reality that you have some control over — your own thoughts, feelings, and behavior — as well as on what you can learn when someone gets triggered in your presence. Trying to control another person's reactivity or opinion of you is a waste of energy. The better plan is to see how reactive incidents can help you understand the deeper layers of your own conditioned mind.

Chapter Three

Learning Your Unique Trigger Signature

Catching the Early Warning Signs

Knowing your trigger signature empowers you to notice the early warning signs that you are triggered or starting to get triggered. Then you'll be able to catch and halt reactivity before doing too much damage.

When you get triggered, you typically react with a set of reactive behaviors, reactive feelings, and reactive thoughts. You may get big and puffed up. Or you may shrink into the woodwork. Your body may get heated up and activated or frozen and shut down. Knowing your trigger signature empowers you to notice the early warning signs that you are triggered or starting to get triggered. Then you'll be able to catch and halt reactivity before doing too much damage.

As I've said, people's trigger reactions tend to be various versions of fight, flight, or freeze. The fight response includes arguing, yelling, and questioning, and these prompt you to *move toward* or *move against* the other in an aggressive or pursuing manner. Flight reactions include defending, explaining, ignoring, and walking out, and these prompt you to *move away* from the other or to *erect some sort of defense* between yourself and the other. The various freeze reactions — such as the deer-in-the-headlights reaction, going blank or numb, smiling robotically — do not move toward, against, or away from. It's as if you are stuck, immobile, checked out, numb, dissociated. Some authors find it useful to add two other types of primitive behaviors to this list: fold and fawn. I consider fold and fawn to be subcategories of the freeze response. *Fold* means you collapse, give up, become passive, or imagine you have no choice but to submit. *Fawn* means you mold your behavior to appease or be less threatening to the perceived aggressor — a robotic smile is one example of this.

Most people can usually identify right away which "F" they tend to favor: fight, flight, or freeze. Consider for yourself: Which F tends to take over your nervous system when you get triggered? Once you identify which F you tend to favor, the next and more useful step is to map a given reactive incident by naming what you actually felt, thought, and did. Let's do this now.

Recall Your Trigger Reactions

Recall a situation where you got triggered: What was the situation, and what actually happened that seemed to set the trigger reaction in motion? Try to recall the location and what the other person did or said. Can you remember any sense of what you felt, what you sensed in your body, and what your thoughts were? Did you have a visible reaction (like walking out), or was it more internal (like going blank)? Review this memory in detail, and jot down one or more feelings (like anger), one or more body sensations (like a tense belly), and one or more thoughts — your reactive story or self-talk (like "No one cares what I have to say"). Then add a description of your inner or outer reaction, such as, "I completely froze, I stopped listening, and I couldn't hear what the person was saying."

Do this type of trigger analysis on at least five different situations where you have gotten triggered. If you want, stop and recall five right now, or if you prefer, make this a journaling assignment for yourself over the next few weeks. Don't necessarily look for incidents that indicate you were triggered. It is often easier to simply recall times you were upset, hurt, angry, frustrated, resentful, confused, numb, overwhelmed, hopeless, disappointed, judgmental, critical, indignant, or shocked. Or recall times you felt betrayed, criticized, ignored, left out, disrespected, alone, attacked, blamed, unimportant, unloved, not needed, not trusted, or not accepted. While feeling ignored, criticized, and so on are really not feelings — they are projections of your core fears onto another's behavior — they are still good places to start this inquiry.

For each instance, recall your internal and outward reactions: Did you yell, blow up, criticize, complain, prod, argue, question, try to ignore it, laugh it off, defend yourself, explain, judge or fume silently, clam up, freeze, give advice, lecture, preach, repeat yourself, threaten, blame, walk out, think vengeful thoughts, plan your escape, fantasize about someone else, vow to stop caring, cry, or get depressed? You can use these words to help you get started as you make a list of your reactive behaviors or trigger reactions.

To illustrate, here is an example of a client named Karen. As the entry point for identifying the elements of her trigger signature, Karen expressed "feeling left out." Karen had just married Tim, who had a fourteen-year-old daughter, Lindsay. Tim had been a single parent for most of Lindsay's life. During their courtship, Karen was often frustrated when Tim and Lindsay had private conversations that seemed to leave her out. She hoped that after marriage, when Karen became Lindsay's stepmom, things would be different. On one particular occasion, about ten months after Tim and Karen were married, Lindsay asked Tim if she could stay overnight at a friend's house on a school night. Tim said yes, and later that evening, he told Karen about his decision. Karen replied: "What about her homework? I thought we agreed that until she gets her grades up, she has to show us she's done her homework every night before bedtime." Karen was angry, disappointed, hurt, and triggered. In the moment, Karen was tempted to bring up her resentment about all the other times Tim had done similar things in the past, but she remained focused on this one incident. Recalling this incident later to identify her trigger signature, she felt some appreciation for herself for not escalating the situation by bringing in her resentments about Tim's past transgressions.

In analyzing the different trigger components, it was easy to identify Karen's *reactive story*: "He puts Lindsay before me.... I'm not important here." Next, she identified her *reactive feelings*: anger, disappointment, hurt, and a touch of self-righteousness. Then she recalled her *body sensations* — a tight jaw, heat in her face. Finally, she recognized that her *reactive behavior* was expressed as a logical argument: "I thought we agreed that she has to show us she's done her homework."

If Karen were to analyze five different triggering episodes, most of them would likely have a similar flavor as the story above:

- Tim letting her down in some way.
- Karen getting angry but trying to do things right — by using reason and logic to argue her point.
- Karen experiencing body sensations associated with high arousal and tension.
- Karen having an internal story that suggests she is not being treated well (not loved, not valued, not important, not considered, left out).

Some of her five episodes might reveal a slightly different set of reactions, but most people only have one or two trigger signatures. If we were to analyze these with great care, we might even see that two seemingly different signatures actually come from the same root fear — like the fear of being unimportant.

Judgmental Thoughts

Some trigger reactions are easy to notice in ourselves and in others — feelings like anger, resentment, and rage. Others are harder to see in others, but fairly easy to notice in ourselves — feelings like hurt, sadness, fear, overwhelm, hopelessness. And some are not even obvious to ourselves — at least, we don't normally think of these as signs of being triggered. In this category are things like having judgmental thoughts or imagining how someone could have or should have behaved. For some people, having judgmental thoughts seems so natural to their personality that they would not categorize this as evidence of being triggered. But I do. I have seen enough during my fifty-five years in this profession to recognize how often people think they are behaving rationally — that their judgments, stories, or interpretations are true or right — when they are actually not seeing the situation clearly because of their triggers. They are viewing "what is" through the lens of one of their core fears, and they don't even realize they have this core fear. Being judgmental toward others as a characteristic stance in life is a good way to avoid facing one's own insecurities.

Treating judgmental thoughts as part of a trigger signature does not necessarily mean that the criticisms are wrong. For instance, in Karen's case, her judgment that Tim was too permissive with Lindsay might be accurate much of the time. This may be one of Tim's personality deficits. But Karen's judgment is still connected to her trigger reaction. She experiences inner pain about Tim's permissiveness because of the meaning she gives to his behavior. By being permissive, Tim seems to value Lindsay's needs over Karen's needs, which is why she believes "I am not a priority." In other words, Karen's judgment reflects her core fear of not being important and her core need to feel included in decisions, that is, to feel like a priority.

In many instances, a critical or judgmental thought arises when we are not feeling emotionally safe in some way, when we fear that one of our core attachment needs is not being met. So our judgment or criticism is a reactive behavior. The other person's behavior has set off this reaction in us. Often we won't notice the emotional reaction underneath our judgmental thought. We may be too caught up in our own fear-story

("I'm not a priority"). Our inner "noticer" doesn't function when we get triggered. But if we pause and get calm, we can intentionally activate our noticer. Then we will see that there is a core fear that needs our compassion.

Distinguishing Intuition from Fear

Trigger reactions can be cloaked in seemingly rational garb. What if your intuition tells you that your romantic partner is having an affair? Say, because your partner comes home later than expected some evening. If you already know that part of your trigger signature is a core fear of abandonment, how do you process this? Should you trust your intuition or treat this feeling as a trigger reaction? The answer is: When your emotional safety is threatened, before focusing on getting "the facts" (grilling your partner over why they were late, and so on), focus first on any reactive feelings that may be underneath the need to know the truth. Pause to notice things like disappointment, hurt feelings, or feeling not valued or not important. Notice memories of or associations to similar feelings in the past. Allow space for whatever feelings or memories arise. If fear or pain arise, let yourself feel soft and tender toward this part of yourself, this fearful or hurting part.

Once you have connected deeply with yourself in this way, then you are in a more openhearted frame of mind, ready to have a conversation with your partner about what happened. In order to openly hear your partner's account, you need to first attend to any fears that have come up in you. But for the purpose of knowing your trigger signature, it's enough just to name your reactive behavior, your reactive feelings and body sensations, your reactive story (or fear-story), your core fear, and your core need. This will help you recognize the possibility that what feels like your intuition might just be your fear-story instead.

Mia and John:
How to Discover One's Trigger Signature

To illustrate how to identify a trigger signature, here is a hypothetical example based on real clients I have worked with.

Mia and John have been dating for six months. They live in different cities, some distance from each other, so they only see each other one week out of every month. In between their in-person visits, they talk almost daily over Zoom or Face-Time. They have an agreement to be sexually monogamous. One of the issues they keep bumping up against is that John likes to report in great detail his activities during the weeks they are apart, and he also wants Mia to share at this level of detail. This helps him feel secure. John grew up with a mother who had a habit of going silent for days if she was unhappy with something he did or said. This felt to young John as if he were being abandoned. Not knowing what was going on for his mother, and suspecting she was holding a grudge against him, he would feel helpless and out of control. John's former girlfriend also had a quiet, somewhat secretive, nature. She wound up having a secret affair, which led to the ending of that relationship. Thus, John carries a fear of abandonment into his relationship with Mia. That's his core fear and primary trigger — fear of being abandoned, fear of someone becoming quiet and cutting off the connection that he depends on to feel safe. If he is aware of his sensitivity regarding silence and secrecy, he can bring a healthy dose of skepticism to any "intuitions" he may have that his girlfriend is keeping secrets or having an affair. He knows this could be his fear talking, rather than his intuition.

Mia isn't comfortable sharing her daily activities in as much detail as John wants. Her communication style is more private, less verbally fluent. She learned as a child that the more she shared honestly about her activities with her mother, the more disapproval she got. Mia recalls telling her mother about her social or romantic life a few times as a young teen. This would be followed by a barrage of accusatory questions from her mother. It seemed like her mother was trying to catch her doing something wrong or did not see Mia as capable of making her own decisions. As this continued, Mia grew more and more sensitive to messages from others that she was bad, wrong, inept, or not good enough. That became her core fear and primary trigger — fear of being (seen as) bad or wrong, fear of someone thinking poorly of her, not seeing her, misjudging her.

Mia and John Get into It

This personality difference leads Mia and John to get into a reactive cycle. On a FaceTime call, John asks Mia, "What have you been up to? Who have you been spending time with?" After a few seconds of silence, she replies, "Oh, I, um, just Vera … and her boyfriend." John feels unsatisfied with her response and wants more information. His internal reactive story is that she's not meeting him in the way he wants to be met, and maybe she never will. He replies, "That's it? Who's the boyfriend? I didn't know she had a boyfriend. Is that new?"

Now, Mia feels pressure in her chest and tightness in her

throat. She thinks to herself: *He's upset with me. What does it take to satisfy this guy?* This is her reactive story. She experiences a slight freeze reaction, but she tries to override this with her familiar lighthearted, almost cheery attitude, saying, "I can't keep up with them — it's been on and off for a while. Now it's on again!" Hearing this, John mistrusts Mia's cheeriness and thinks, *I wonder if this guy is attracted to Mia, and is Mia attracted to him?* But he says, "Are you alright? You sound nervous." This question sends Mia into a full-blown trigger reaction, and she responds, "Am I alright? Am I alright? What are you talking about? Why wouldn't I be alright?!" Hearing this, John responds in anger: "I knew there was more to this. You're trying to protect something. Why won't you just answer my question?!"

John's Trigger Signature

This is just one of several similar exchanges between John and Mia, but from this, we can generalize John's trigger signature.

1. John's *core fear* is his fear of abandonment, which he has encountered before in earlier relationships. By the time he meets Mia, he already knows this about himself, including how it feels to get triggered. Part of his trigger signature is a familiar sense of feeling alone, not responded to, not cared about, not met.

2. John's *reactive story* is that Mia is not meeting him and perhaps cannot meet him. This is reflected in John's self-talk, which is another aspect of his trigger signature. He tends to focus on what the other person is *not* doing, such as the story that someone

is not "there for him." Knowing this, John can learn
to be on the lookout for such self-talk.

3. John's *reactive feelings* tend to be anger or irritation,
and this is useful information about his trigger
signature. He can use that to help identify what's
going on: *If I'm feeling angry or irritated, I am probably triggered.*

4. The *body sensations* that accompany John's self-talk
and anger are a sense of being empty or hungry, a
sense that he is losing something, and a sense that
someone is moving away from him. He also often
feels a subtle body impulse to pursue or go after
Mia. Ultimately, he can add these reactive body
sensations to his list of "Signs I Am Triggered."

Once John identifies all of these aspects to his trigger signature, he can use them as "early warning signs" of being triggered. In fact, if he notices even *one* of these reactions, he can
know he is probably triggered, and it's better if he doesn't wait
till all his typical trigger reactions appear. Some people are most
attuned to thoughts and less aware of body sensations, so these
people need to be on the lookout for thoughts, interpretations,
assumptions, suspicions, fear-stories, or self-talk that point to
the underlying core fear. Others find it easier to notice feelings,
and still others, body sensations. For most people, thoughts
are the most misleading, often causing them to think they're
being rational or objective when they're not. Thoughts come
from the ego-mind, and the ego-mind is in the habit of making
reasonable-sounding justifications — making sense of events in
a way that leaves the person's self-image intact and unblemished.
Be on the lookout for self-justifying stories! Everyone does this
at times, and it's a sign that you're triggered.

Mia's Trigger Signature

Based on the interaction described above, we can also identify the main elements of Mia's trigger signature. Let's review the indicators:

1. Mia's *core fear* is that she is not good enough, and her tendency is to react when she thinks she is being judged, criticized, misunderstood, or seen as bad, wrong, untrustworthy, or incapable. In contrast to John, she is not so worried about whether she is loved, but rather whether she is seen as a good, worthy, capable person. It's important to remember that not everyone has the same core fears. Sure, we all want to be loved, respected, and thought well of, but our deepest insecurities are related to which of these needs were most frustrated in our formative years. Like John, Mia has encountered her own core fear in earlier relationships, so she already has this knowledge about herself.

2. Mia's *reactive story* is reflected in her self-talk: *He's upset with me. What does it take to satisfy this guy?* Such self-talk reveals Mia's tendency to distance herself from her core fear of not being enough by judging John as hard to satisfy.

3. When Mia gets triggered, her *reactive feelings* include two impulses: wanting to get away and wanting to push back in self-defense. At times, she also has the impulse to just give up. Not talking at all is one of her go-to strategies for staying safe. What is most apparent in this encounter, though, is her angry, defensive, raised-voice comment, "Am I alright? Why wouldn't

I be alright?!" With this aggressive outburst, Mia can clearly see she is in a triggered state.

4. After John's opening questions, "What have you been up to? Who have you been spending time with?" Mia's reactive *body sensations* include feeling tense and guarded. She notices a tightness in her throat and chest. John's questions alone are enough to trigger her to feel uncomfortable and experience a freeze-type bodily reaction. With practice, she can learn to recognize her attempt to override these sensations as a sign of being triggered.

Ultimately, if Mia shows any one of these indicators, she is triggered. She doesn't need to wait for all of them to appear. It's good to be aware of all of these early warning signs, though, because most people can only notice one or two at a time.

Identify Your Unique Trigger Signature

Knowing your trigger signature helps you prevent needless heartache and conflict because it allows you to:

1. Pause in the middle of being triggered and stop talking, stop typing, stop imagining things, and stop walking out the door.
2. Recognize that being triggered is not the time to send that email rant, quit your job, or tell your spouse, "I want a divorce."
3. Avoid doing damage to a relationship by triggering another person or adding fuel to the fire.
4. Avoid doing damage to yourself by halting self-destructive actions and thoughts.

Take time now to consider your own trigger signature more closely. Think about one of the trigger episodes that you recalled earlier, and consider what core fear, reactive story, reactive feelings, and reactive body sensations it includes. It's not necessary to identify everything. As I note in John and Mia's example, we only need to notice one cue to know we are triggered or starting to get triggered. What is one of your most recognizable cues? Do you raise your voice, feel a hollow sensation in your chest, or have difficulty breathing? Do you feel slightly numb or try to justify yourself with reasoned arguments? Are you being reasonable as a defense?

It also can help to identify whether your larger tendency is to engage fight, flight, or freeze when you get triggered. Each of the three Fs have their own characteristics and typical reactive behaviors. Fight is characterized by feelings like anger, irritation, annoyance; self-talk that is judgmental, accusatory, blaming, or critical; and sensations like clenched fists or jaw, a knot in the stomach, energy running up the back, and heat in the face; and impulses to move against or to pursue. Flight is more likely to bring up feelings like sadness, panic, anxiety, fear, and hopelessness; self-talk that is defensive, explanatory, self-justifying, or that tries to figure out how to change or avoid the situation; sensations like heaviness in the chest, tightness in the throat, increased tension in the eyes or head, or agitation; and impulses to move, such as wanting to run away or hide. Freeze is best described as a deer-in-the-headlights reaction. Freeze brings up feelings like confusion, overwhelm, shock, going blank, being emotionally shut down, and dissociating; self-talk like *What's happening? I don't know what to do. How did I get here?*; sensations like numbness or not feeling anything; and involuntary actions like shaking or self-soothing movements such as rubbing two fingers together.

As you consider your own trigger signature, be compassionate with yourself. This sort of inquiry takes a certain degree of humility. The wish for self-knowledge needs to be greater than the need to look good. The first step in recognizing your trigger signature is to simply accept that you do get triggered. In fact, part of noticing you are triggered can be recognizing that you tend to blame others for your own reactions, that your pride sometimes won't let you acknowledge your own fear-stories, and that you believe there's something wrong or crazy about getting triggered. If you have shame or self-criticism toward yourself when you're triggered, pause for a moment and see if you can step outside of and above yourself — sort of like watching yourself in a movie. See this person who is having self-deprecating judgments about being triggered. Notice the internal beliefs that are triggered that make this person feel unlovable. How does it feel watching this person as if they were in a movie? Do you identify with the judgmental inner critic or with the person being judged? Or do you feel more like an impartial witness of the whole scene — separate from the conflicting parts inside this person? What is your overall feeling watching this movie?

Acceptance of your triggers might not come easily. You may need to first accept this fact. You might have to accept that you feel shame, self-judgment, or contempt toward the triggered part of yourself. This really is an okay place to be. The road to getting somewhere new in yourself, perhaps to somewhere more loving or self-forgiving, always starts with being where you are now. Indeed, "being where you are" is a theme in this work and in this book.

Chapter Four

Pausing to Regulate Yourself

Restoring an Inner Sense of Safety

Pausing is important because it stops you from doing or saying things that might escalate a conflict, retraumatize yourself or another person, or cause some other kind of harm.

A trigger reaction can be like a runaway freight train. Once it is set in motion, it is not easy to stop. Without the ability to put on the brakes, it can do a lot of damage. So we need to develop our inner braking system, which includes noticing one or more aspects of our trigger signature and stopping whatever we are doing, and even what we're thinking, right away. This is not easy. It takes practice. And in the beginning you will probably fail to stop soon enough more often than you will succeed.

Pausing is important because it stops you from doing or saying things that might escalate a conflict, retraumatize yourself or another person, or cause some other kind of harm.

Remember, when our animal instincts take over, anything goes. We may react to harsh voice tones or insensitive words as if the other person were an enemy who was attacking us. People who go into a blind rage have been triggered, and no good ever comes from such a state.

The other reason to pause is because it helps you develop voluntary control over your internal reactive states. You learn to insert a conscious choice into what otherwise would be an automatic sequence of primitive behaviors (fight, flight, or freeze). With practice, you can learn to interrupt your animal instincts. This allows you to slow everything down — to consciously breathe more slowly and to quiet your racing thoughts.

Stopping is difficult at first because the neurochemical reactions that get triggered in the nervous system have tremendous force and power. These reactions are part of our original physical survival mechanism. They override and overpower our ability to reason, to weigh options, to think things through.

How can we learn to pause so we can slow down our runaway reactions? We learn through conscious effort and through believing we can. In the Five Steps of Trigger Work, pausing to self-regulate is the third step. The exercises in this chapter help you to practice pausing and calming, but the other exercises in this book are part of this work, too. The more you accept and learn to recognize triggers, the easier it is to pause, and after you get calm, you can discover the greater rewards in store (as later chapters show).

What Does It Mean to Pause?

Mastering the art of pausing involves noticing that one of your early warning signs is happening, and then, without thinking much about it, you stop what you are doing. You might silently say "pause" or create some other signal that reminds you to stop reacting. This "other signal" could be a different word, perhaps one that has always signaled safety for you, or maybe you can use a physical gesture as your wake-up call — like touching the body part where you notice reactive sensations or putting your hand over your mouth as a reminder to shut up.

Make an agreement with yourself to use this signal at the first sign of reactivity. Even if you miss the first sign, and reactivity goes on for a while, pause as soon as you can. Late is better than never. Late is actually the best most people can accomplish.

Most of the time, trigger reactions occur in the presence of another person, so it can also be helpful to make a pause agreement with others. Ideally, you and this other person would discuss the value of pausing when triggered and come to a mutual agreement that if either person uses a pause signal — whether that's the word "pause" or something else — both people will stop what they are doing and saying. No explanation needed; everything stops. Of course, successfully pausing in the middle of an argument is a lot easier if both people have already agreed to do this.

Creating a Pause Agreement with Others

The first part of creating a pause agreement with others is to decide that this is a good thing to do — everyone should see the value of halting reactive behavior before too much damage gets done (see chapter 7 for more on pausing with an intimate partner). Then you decide together on a word or simple phrase that is easy to remember and does not have negative associations. The word "stop," for example, may seem quite functional, but many people find this word comes with a lot of baggage; they associate it with being told to stop certain behaviors as kids. "Time-out" is another popular phrase that works for some but not for others. The word "pause" is often chosen because it's neutral, but in the end, the only important thing is that everyone agree on the pause signal.

In addition, whatever word is used, try to say this in a neutral voice tone, or better yet, a friendly tone. This can be hard at first, but this will come with practice. With practice comes skillfulness. With skillfulness comes more ease. With ease comes friendliness.

The main aspect of the pause agreement is that, if anyone gives the pause signal, everyone stops talking immediately. You don't even finish what you were saying. The purpose of this pause is not to get someone to shut up, even though this may be a useful by-product. You pause in order to give everyone time to get calm and reassure themselves that they are not in any real danger. You also use the pause to bring empathy and compassion to yourself. This self-compassion aspect of the pause is discussed in the next chapter.

The final aspect of the agreement is to decide how long to pause before trying to verbally connect again. How long will it take for everyone to become calm and openhearted enough to engage in a repair? In a dyad or two-person relationship, like an intimate couple, the best practice involves a two-stage process. First, when someone gives the pause signal, both people stop talking and take ten slow deep breaths. Second, assuming the ten breaths have helped, you consider together whether the pause should be short (ten to fifteen minutes), medium (one to three hours), or long (three to eight hours). If the pause is going to be fifteen minutes or more, people generally will move to different rooms or locations. While no one can know exactly how long you each will need, the short-medium-long time estimate gives you something to shoot for. It affirms your intention to come back and repair, rather than just dropping the matter and hoping it'll go away. This time agreement tells you when you will check back with each other to ask, "Are we ready to move ahead to repair what just happened, or does one of us need more time?" (The repair process is described in chapter 6.) If someone needs more time, then you briefly discuss how long you will take before checking back with each other again to repair.

There is no perfect formula for deciding how long to pause. But with a little practice and experience, plus a measure of goodwill, the process starts to work more smoothly. The main pitfall is that one person may get retriggered if the other person does not come back to check in as expected. If this happens, the person may need to extend their own pause time to work with this additional trigger reaction.

In groups (that is, any situation with more than two people), the pause-agreement procedure is a little different, and this is described in chapters 10 and 11.

Conscious Self-Calming

The very act of saying or hearing the word "pause" will bring a bit of self-awareness back. Then it's time to do a self-calming practice for at least three minutes, probably more. Intentionally watching and slowing your breathing is a time-honored practice for calming the human nervous system.

Use the following breathing exercise during a pause, but I recommend first practicing this when you are not triggered.

Then you'll have easier access to it when you do get triggered: Find a safe, comfortable place to sit or lie down. Close your eyes if this feels natural and good. While breathing through your nose, try putting your attention on the body sensations of your breath coming in and going out. Start by just noticing. Do this for a while. Then make your breathing slower and deeper, imagining your whole torso as a balloon that expands with the in-breath and lets go and relaxes with the out-breath. Rest a bit at the end of each out-breath. Do this for a while. Focus attention on lengthening the out-breath, feeling yourself relaxing more and more with every exhale, letting go of tension, letting go of thoughts. Many find that an ideal rhythm is to breathe in for four counts and out for six to eight. Brain scientists have found that this rhythm activates the vagus nerve, which then releases relaxation hormones throughout the body. But even if you only rest a little bit at the end of the out-breath, the relaxation effect will be similar.

When reactive thoughts enter your mind and take your focus away from your breath, do not resist or make a problem out of this. Simply bring your attention gently back to the body sensations of breathing. Feel your torso and belly expand as you inhale. Feel your chest and shoulders relaxing as you exhale. Feel the muscles of your face and jaw relax as you exhale. Scan your body for areas where you are holding tension, and see if you can bring more spaciousness to these areas by imagining that you are breathing into these places.

This conscious self-calming practice should be used during your pause time. You pause in order to stop further damage to your sense of safety and connection, but you are also pausing to give yourself time to calm your nervous system so your higher brain functioning can come back online. Knowing how to self-regulate is a vital skill for your health and well-being.

Once you are calm, and your whole system feels grounded in the present moment, then you are no longer at the mercy of your reptile brain. Now you can calmly assess the situation, or any damage that has been caused, with your higher brain's full resources available. Now you can spend some time digesting what you have just experienced and inquiring into how your trigger reaction may be connected to past trauma or unfinished emotional business. This inquiry process is the subject of the next chapter, which describes how to use any trigger reaction as a doorway to healing past wounds and trauma. This is one of the most important benefits of pausing to self-regulate — it opens the way for self-healing through self-compassion.

Other Self-Calming Techniques

One other popular and effective calming practice is to focus your attention on how your body feels sitting in, and being supported by, a chair. To practice this exercise in the absence of a triggering event, find a chair to sit on where you feel comfortable and safe. Close your eyes and pay attention to the sensations of your rear end on the chair, and perhaps also the sensations of your arms resting on the arms of the chair. Notice your breath going in and out, as above. Breathe slowly through your nose, with special attention to letting go and relaxing with each exhale. Feel yourself sinking into the chair, letting go into gravity, as you notice how the chair holds and supports you. With each exhalation, let go a bit more into being held by the chair. Notice how it feels to allow your weight to be held and supported.

In addition, any meditation practice for moving beyond personality patterns and mind chatter is helpful during a pause. If you already have a practice that works, use that.

Some people find it difficult to notice body sensations, so for these people, counting to ten, twenty, or one hundred can work well. Or you may like using a mantra — a word or set of words designed to help the mind focus, stabilize, or settle down. Mantras often work well for people who are not so in touch with the body.

Tapping or EMDR (eye movement desensitization and reprocessing) can also be useful. So can disciplines like yoga, tai chi, chi gung, chanting, or doing a rosary. Some people find it helpful to really get into their bodies through running, walking, dancing, or lifting weights. Experiment to discover what works best for you.

Learning from Past Mistakes

People can get frustrated and feel like giving up when they forget to pause or don't initiate a pause soon enough. If this happens to you at first, don't give up. The best way to shorten the time lag between when you first become reactive and when you actually pause is to use your past failures as opportunities for learning. Here's an exercise to help you do that:

First, recall an interpersonal triggering episode where both people were triggered and you did not pause. Identify why you did not pause. Maybe one person said "pause," and this was ignored. Maybe you thought about calling for a pause but were afraid this might make things worse. Maybe things got so frustrating that you both walked out. Whatever the reason, just naming it now can help you accept that resistance to change is common. It is not easy to adopt a new habit just because you know it's a good idea. Naming your reason for not pausing gives you insight into your personal fears and resistances. Try to accept your resistance. Paradoxically, noticing and accepting resistance helps you overcome it. This seems to be a law of human nature: Don't resist your resistance. Accept and inquire into your resistance, listen to what it is telling you, and it will soon fall away. (To be clear, this is resistance to learning something new and useful, not the type of healthy resistance related to asserting authentic boundaries.)

As you recall this incident, consider if there was already some tension between the two of you, even before anyone got noticeably triggered. Was there an earlier event or conversation that never felt complete or never got resolved? Was there a conversation that needed to happen and didn't? If so, and you could do things over, how and when might you have initiated this conversation with the other person? In your mind right now, as part of this exercise, say the exact words you could have said to start that conversation. Ask yourself, "How do I wish I had responded, if I could do it over?" Imagine yourself delivering this more self-aware or courageous response. Doing so will prepare you to do a better job next time this sort of situation presents itself.

Then bring to mind what you felt, sensed, said, or thought that indicated you were getting triggered. In retrospect, which elements of your trigger signature were present or visible to you? Recall, in as much detail as you can, what was going on when you noticed these indicators. Identify the moment in this sequence of events when you should have paused. Imagine yourself feeling whatever you felt when you were triggered and still managing to say "pause." Using your imagination, feel how this feels. Do you feel scared, robotic, phony, agitated, angry? Just accept whatever is true.

But what if you did say "pause," and your invitation to

pause was ignored? If this happened, review how you spoke. Can you sense how your throat felt? How your voice sounded? How the rest of your body felt? Take some time to reflect on this. Can you see anything you weren't aware of at the time? Maybe you did not actually say "pause" — maybe you used a different word. Maybe, without being aware of it, you used more words than you needed to. Or maybe your voice was so constricted that the words were hardly audible. There are many reasons that a pause attempt might get ignored without it being anyone's fault. After all, you were both triggered! In real life, speaking over another person's words may be difficult, so go back in your mind's eye and imagine yourself saying "pause" repeatedly in a neutral tone of voice, sort of like a broken record, until the other person stops talking. It might not always work in real life, but do this broken-record exercise anyway. It trains you to be able to firmly mark a boundary — even under fire.

Sometimes a conflict or episode ends when one person walks out or leaves. If this is what happened, and it was done in anger or frustration, it doesn't really qualify as a pause; it would be considered a reaction. So recall the scenario and remember how the walkout occurred — who did or said what, and how did this feel to you? Take time to review this in your mind's eye. Each time you review past events in one of these skill exercises, the purpose is to see if you can notice more of what happened than you did when the sparks were flying. Usually, people can see a lot more in hindsight because, during reflection, they feel calm and safe.

However, if you get retriggered while doing one of these self-reflection exercises, take a pause and do some conscious breathing. One indicator that you are starting to get retriggered is when something like this happens: While reviewing an incident, you remember how helpless or ineffectual you felt. This may bring up reactive feelings like anger and reactive thoughts like blaming. Or it may bring up memories of times your core needs to feel valued and respected were not met. If you find yourself triggered like this, pause and calm yourself, and spend some time being with your tender, hurting feelings with gentleness and self-compassion. The next chapter provides more practices for accessing and deepening self-compassion.

Once you have done a thorough reflection of what occurred when your pause attempt was not honored, go through the memory again and imagine yourself telling the other person that you are now going to exit the situation. Find a way to do this using a few neutral words. You might say, for example, "I need to take a break. I'll be back." Create a brief script for yourself and imagine saying this, even if the other person is still in the middle of speaking. Notice how you feel while saying it and right after saying it. Sit with this a moment. See if you can appreciate yourself for having the courage to mark a boundary for the good of both of you. Now imagine yourself speaking this statement several more times while imagining yourself leaving the room. Of course, in the original situation, leaving might not be an option; you might have been in a moving automobile or on an airplane. In that case, imagine saying that you are going to meditate, pray, or "go inside," and while sitting next to your partner, imagine going inward and doing slow conscious breathing.

One thing most people realize when they do this self-reflection exercise is that there were many moments when they could have paused, but they held off in hopes that the conversation would soon take a turn for the better. People think: *If*

I can just get my partner to hear this one thing, then they'll understand. As you do this exercise, watch for thoughts like that, and admit this is probably wishful thinking. The main objective to this exercise is to train yourself to see that you actually can observe a trigger reaction in the making, notice elements of your trigger signature, and signal for a pause when you need to. This exercise also often reveals how pausing sooner rather than later means there is less damage to repair later on.

If the Other Person Is Triggered and Cannot Pause

Sometimes, or in some situations, you will recognize that the other person is triggered before you notice this in yourself. Maybe you are wired to react less intensely, or maybe your reactions build more slowly. This can be a gift to your partner and others because this means you are better able to notice and halt reactivity before it escalates. In this case, give the pause signal the same way you would if you noticed your own reactivity. However, don't say, "You're triggered. We need to pause." Just say "pause" or "I need to pause."

If you find yourself with someone who gets triggered and cannot or will not pause, try to view this as another opportunity for inner work. There is something you are here to learn in this relationship that may have to do with accepting that sometimes you have to mark a boundary or do things that displease someone you care about — not an easy assignment. You may need to take a unilateral pause and remove yourself. Otherwise, you might feel trapped and could grow to resent your partner.

Remember, some people carry so much trauma, shame, or insecurity inside that their nervous system is perpetually on high alert. Some find it nearly impossible to initiate a pause or to stop reacting no matter how many times you ask. Even if you have a prior pause agreement, the other person may keep reacting (talking, arguing, trying to be right), or they may become triggered by your request to pause.

If this happens, you could say, "I need to pause. I'd like to calm myself and come back to this after dinner." Ideally, you will be able to say this in a warm or soothing tone of voice, and you might add a note of reassurance, such as, "I know we'll get through this," or "I promise to come and find you after I'm calm."

If you do this consistently — initiating a unilateral pause, during which you do self-calming practices — this will influence your relationship for the better because this represents you taking care of yourself by speaking up and maintaining a self-respecting boundary. You are affirming your unwillingness to participate in unproductive and damaging vicious cycles. You are unwilling to receive or listen to the other person's acting-out behavior. This is a healthy boundary. People who tend to be codependent often find this unilateral pause practice especially helpful. It gives them practice standing firm and setting healthy boundaries, even at the risk of upsetting a partner. Remember, upsets can be repaired.

When we treat ourselves in a more self-respecting way, this affects how others relate to us. Also, pausing and exiting the situation forces the other person to do something different than what they have done in the past. We can't be sure how the other will use this time, but a unilateral pause means the other person can't continue arguing, defending, questioning, blaming, and so on. Maybe they will discover new resources within themselves for dealing with their upset feelings.

Of course, if you're in a situation where you have made a pause agreement with a partner, and it rarely works, you may need to accept that you do not really have a viable agreement. Your best option is to continue asking for a pause when you notice yourself or the other becoming triggered, and if the other keeps reacting, take a unilateral pause.

Practice Pausing Before You Need It

Learning to pause takes commitment and discipline. The best way to learn this practice is to make an agreement with a partner, a friend, or even with a group to say "pause" during any conversation that gets even a little bit intense, fast-paced, or convoluted. It may not mean that anyone is triggered. It's really just for practice. When you do this, you may find that people really do appreciate the opportunity to pause and check in on the state of their nervous system from time to time. And they may realize they were actually triggered. Often, a person will not recognize when they are triggered because they have gotten used to living with a certain level of fear or anxiety.

This type of just-for-practice pause can be especially useful if one person speaks and thinks a lot faster than the other person. If this is beneficial in your primary partnership or in a business relationship, you might want to use a different word than "pause," especially if you are also using the word "pause" to halt trigger reactions. I suggest phrases like "Can we slow this down?" or "I'd like to stop the action for a moment and check in." These phrases can work well in both business and intimate relationships.

In some of the personal growth groups and social meditation groups I lead, I simply ring a little chime at random intervals or when things are getting intense. The group agrees to pause, get silent, and look inward whenever they hear this chime. For some, it is an opportunity to become calm, to relax, or to feel the ground beneath them. Others use the pause to check in and notice feelings and thoughts. Before the group interaction resumes, people often like to share what they became aware of during their pause.

Aside from its usefulness as a practice for halting reactivity, inserting a pause as a mindfulness break at various points in your daily routine can reduce your stress and increase your connection to yourself and others. Too many of us go through our lives on autopilot, speaking and acting from habit rather than from authentic awareness. But if we get into the habit of quickly pausing to check in with ourselves every time we open our mouth to speak, it allows us to bring more of our whole self, more awareness of layers and nuances, into our communications with others.

Chapter Five

Being with Sensations and Emotions

Becoming a Spacious, Loving Presence

*Whatever you notice arising in you, see if you can
welcome this and embrace it.*

This chapter describes how to work with trigger reactions in a way that creates a corrective emotional experience. Instead of feeling like we are lacking in some way, we gain a greater sense of wholeness through discovering aspects of ourselves that have been hiding in the shadows. As we explore the dark recesses of our unconscious mind, we gently bring these hidden aspects into the light.

The first part of this chapter provides a guided tour of what all children need to grow up into healthy, secure adults. These exercises bring us into a more loving and supportive relationship with ourselves. Then we will learn some self-compassion practices to use during our pause or whenever we get triggered.

Inner Work: Approaching Life as a Practice

Trigger reactions help us see where our childhood unfinished business is. Underneath such reactions are buried fears and buried pain that need attention and tenderness. Sometimes there are feelings we never felt safe to feel or attachment needs we never felt safe to express.

I have always liked the phrase "daily life as spiritual practice." This phrase reminds me that we can approach everything that happens in life as an opportunity for inner work — for developing into a more enlightened human being, expanding our sense of identity to include not just our own self-interest but "the good of the whole." For me, personally, this inner work has taken the form of noticing whenever I feel resistance to *what is*. Resistance to what is almost always indicates some fear of emotional discomfort. This is a type of trigger reaction. When I notice my own resistance, I take this as a sign that there is inside me some buried pain, unhealed wound, or developmental deficit that I have not fully owned, accepted, embraced, and loved. Like most people, I instinctively resist having to face and deal with feelings or fears that are uncomfortable. So the only thing that gets me to look into these uncomfortable areas is my commitment to "life as a practice."

Fear of Being Weak or Needy

As children, we may have been criticized or shamed when we expressed our tears, fears, hurts, or needs. Maybe we were laughed at or ridiculed. Maybe we were told it's wrong to be selfish or weak. Maybe someone labeled us too sensitive or too emotional. Our ordinary upsets or weaknesses may have made adults uncomfortable, perhaps triggering their own fears that if their child was unhappy or imperfect, this meant they were not a good enough parent. Such common parental fears and self-doubts can spill out onto their children — creating the impression in the child's mind that *If I am in need or in pain, no one wants to be around me or people get upset. Maybe I'm bad or wrong when I feel such things.*

Pause now as you're reading this. Does any of this apply to you? Allow yourself some space to experience whatever feelings, sensations, memories, or thoughts may be arising in you. Personally, as I was writing these words about parents being anxious around children's upset feelings, I felt sadness and a slight achy sensation in my chest. I know that this was true of my parents, especially my father.

Whatever you notice arising in you, see if you can welcome this and embrace it. By allowing yourself to feel something that was not allowed in the past, you take a small step toward inner healing. You begin the process of reclaiming your lost, rejected, or abandoned parts.

Childhood Attachment Needs

In order to develop into a fully functioning, securely attached adult, certain childhood needs must be met. Almost everyone experiences some frustration of these needs.

During infancy, children need touch, eye contact, and soothing voice tones from their caregivers. Children need to be picked up and lovingly held when they are distressed. This is called coregulation. We never outgrow this need for coregulation, but in infancy, we need it for our survival and for the proper development of our nervous systems.

All children need to feel safe and protected from physical and emotional harm. Did you feel protected as a child? Or were you often left to deal with scary or dangerous things on your own? Was your parents' behavior sometimes frightening to you? Do you recall anyone holding you and comforting you while you cried? Was there a trusted adult that you ran to for safety or comfort when you were afraid? Pause now to reflect on these questions. Notice any body sensations, feelings, or thoughts that come up. Consider how you feel about what you notice. For example, if you notice feelings of sadness about something you recall, how do you feel about noticing your sadness? Can you accept that you felt this way, or do you judge yourself? There is no right or wrong answer to any of these questions. The idea is to be curious and to improve your ability to uncover hidden feelings.

All children need loving attention. Children need to feel loved, cherished, and valued. They need quality time with a parent who gives them undivided attention, both to notice if the child seems distressed and to listen to the child and show interest in what the child is interested in. Did you feel loved in this way? Did your parents seem to enjoy spending time with you? Or did they spend time with you, but their attention was divided, giving you the impression that they were just putting in their time without having a genuine interest in you? Pause now to reflect on these questions. Notice any body sensations, feelings, or thoughts that come up, and notice how you feel about what you notice.

All children need supportive guidance. Children need adults to show them how to do things, like throwing a ball or swimming. They need help learning patience, learning that sometimes you have to apply effort for a long time before you can enjoy rewarding results. They need help learning how to communicate and put their feelings into words. They also need the space to try new things on their own, like learning to pound a nail with a hammer — without the adult taking over. They need guidance, but they also need to be trusted to do things without undue adult interference. How was your childhood in this regard? Did anyone ever patiently show you how to do a new task? Can you remember how that felt? Guidance is something many of us get from someone other than a parent — like a coach or teacher. As you reflect on your childhood, recall any times when you wanted guidance but didn't get it — either because you did not feel safe to ask or because it was clearly not available. Do you recall a parent interfering with your efforts to master a task or do something by yourself? Are your memories of receiving guidance mostly positive? Pause to reflect on these questions, notice any body sensations and feelings that come up, and notice how you feel about what you notice.

Exercise: Compassion for Your Inner Child

When you take time to reflect on how protected, loved, and respected you felt as a child, this strengthens your capacity for self-compassion. Here is an exercise for fostering that compassion directly. It starts with recalling an incident, a memory, or a period of time during your earlier life when one of your important developmental needs was not met (such as an event or situation you recalled in the previous section). Or maybe you do not have any specific memories, but you have an intuition, or an overall felt-sense, that a particular need was frustrated.

Pick something that was emotionally hurtful, but do not pick anything where your physical body was violated or you experienced physical aggression (like someone hitting you) or when you feared for your (or someone else's) physical safety. This exercise is meant to be something you can do safely without a therapist or coach, so don't pick something that was deeply traumatic or likely to trigger intense feelings.

Being with a Painful Memory

Once you have a memory or need in mind, find a safe, comfortable place to sit or lie down where you will not be interrupted. Set aside at least thirty minutes, so your mind can be free from other commitments. Only do this when you know you will have enough time and attention to fully focus.

When you are ready to begin, relax your body, and calm your nervous system. Feel your body relaxing into the chair or the floor. Allow your breathing to slow down as you sense the air going in and out. Rest for a while at the end of each exhale. Take some time like this, just sensing your breath and the rise and fall of your belly or torso. When you feel ready, allow your attention to move to the childhood memory when something happened that made you feel unloved, criticized, neglected, abandoned, rejected, misunderstood, alone, or overwhelmed.

Take time to replay the movie of this scene in your mind, as you breathe slowly and attend spaciously, seeing all this from a big-picture perspective — viewing the elements in the scene as if you were in the audience watching a movie, as if it is happening right before your eyes.

Next, bring your attention to this younger version of you. Imagine or recall what this younger you was feeling, thinking, or wanting. As the audience, see if you can take the posture of an open, spacious, loving witness. Continue to breathe fully in order to activate enough self-support to hold whatever feelings may come up. As you observe this younger you on the movie screen of your imagination, see if you can feel empathy for this younger you. Feel what this child felt while also maintaining the position of the witness or observer. What do you feel as the observer? At this point, your attention is on yourself as the witness while at the same time feeling empathy with the younger you in the movie scene. You adopt a dual focus of attention — you are the audience as well as the star of the movie, and you are aware at both levels. Stay with this for a while.

As an aside: If you find this hard to visualize, you can also do this exercise in writing — describing through words on a page the sequence of events, the feelings you recall having, and how it feels to observe this younger you.

As the witness or narrator of this scene, what body sensations come up? What feelings? Do you feel moved to tears? Do you feel love? Do you feel sadness or pain? Can you feel tenderness, empathy, or compassion for the younger you? Do you feel any anger or a desire to protect this young person? What other thoughts come up? Is there anything you wish you could say to anyone in the scene — to your younger self or to another person who is there? Take your time to allow images and feelings to arise and to change, move, expand, or recede as they will. Stay open and curious. Just see what happens next, while tracking your body sensations and feelings. Keep coming back to noticing your breathing.

If feelings ever get too intense, or if you start to go blank or numb, back off from this experience by opening your eyes and looking around. Look at some of the objects in the room you are in. Name something specific about one of the objects (such as, "I see a yellow-and-red painting with a gold frame"). When you feel calm again, bring yourself gently back to being the witness of this childhood scene. Be sure your breathing remains slow, even, and relaxed — creating a comforting rhythm, sort of like the ebb and flow of ocean waves.

If it feels natural, imagine reaching out to this inner child, opening your arms, bringing this child close to you, and holding and comforting your tender self as someone you love very much. Stay with this for a while, as you offer your reassuring presence to this child — as if to say, "You are safe now. Whatever you are feeling is okay. I am here with you. You are not alone."

When you feel ready to bring this inner exploration to a close, open your eyes and look around the room. If you are lying down, sit up again. Pick an object in the room to focus on for a moment. Feel the sensations of your butt on the chair or your feet on the floor. Move your body with the intent to activate your connection to the outer world. Offer yourself appreciation for being willing to step into the unknown to discover hidden aspects of yourself and your history.

Debriefing the Exercise

Either immediately afterward or later, consider what the exercise was like for you. Reflect on the experience itself. The main purpose of this exercise is to strengthen your awareness and self-compassion muscles, but some people find that this exercise helps them uncover deeply buried memories or heal old wounds. The exercises in this book provide various ways to activate more mindfulness, self-acceptance, self-empathy, and self-compassion. Some activities will work well for you, and some may not. If you find a particular exercise to be beneficial, I suggest you record the instructions on a voice recorder, pausing for several seconds between each prompt or question, so you can sit back and repeat the exercise later while simply listening to the recorded instructions, rather than reading along.

This compassion exercise can be especially useful for people who are accustomed to seeing themselves as strong, thick-skinned, self-reliant, or unflappable. Such a self-image could indicate that someone "hasn't got time for the pain." Maybe they even judge people who spend too much time in self-pity or victimhood. The exercise might also be helpful for those who judge or want to get rid of the parts of themselves that (they believe) make them unattractive to others — things like emotional sensitivity or reactivity. The truth is everyone has within them a reservoir of unfelt fear or pain, which causes some portion of their energy or their attention to be stuck or frozen in the past. Tenderness or compassion toward a hurting inner child will help to unfreeze this stuckness and allow your life energy to move once again. At first, this movement of energy might seem scary or unnatural — like when a person starts sobbing, shaking, or trembling as old memories surface. But movements like these are a sign that healing and integration are taking place. Be sure to offer reassurance and comfort to yourself if such things occur.

Emily Practices Compassion for Her Inner Child

Emily made her living as a personal coach for executives, so she thought she was pretty familiar with the hidden layers of the human personality. She was accustomed to people being vulnerable with her, but she was not so comfortable showing her own fears and insecurities to others. When she came to see me for coaching, she said she was having difficulty creating a feeling of mutual connection with her husband of ten years, David. In particular, she described a triggering incident that happened when she tried to get close to David by asking him how he was doing.

As we discussed this, Emily was reminded of numerous childhood incidents where her father was willing to spend time with her, but only on his terms. He took her to the racetrack with him — even though she never had much interest in horses or racing. He brought her with him to the building supply store, and he watched sports on TV with her. None of these activities interested her, but it was difficult to get time with her dad, so she took what she could get.

I guided Emily to do the Compassion for Your Inner Child exercise. As she got in touch with the memory of how she felt sitting next to her dad at the racetrack, she said: "I felt like there was a big hole in the middle of my chest. There was this empty place inside. Yes. I felt empty… adrift… untethered… not connected to anything." I invited her to attend to her breathing and to make space for these feelings and sensations. She noticed her body stiffening up — as if she was resisting being with these sensations. "They make me feel so weak," she reported. "Like I'm nothing without my connection to him… like I don't exist. I do not want to be that dependent on someone else." She sat for a while feeling both the emptiness inside and the wish to push this feeling away. I reminded her to just be with whatever was coming up. In this exercise, there's no place we are supposed to get to.

After a while her body began to vibrate up and down a little, as if she was riding on a bumpy road. She had the impulse to grab herself, wrapping her two arms around her torso. The vibrating continued for a few seconds and then became still. Tears began to flow from her eyes. Still holding herself, her body softened. She reported, "Something changed when I started to embrace my body like this. It seemed like someone heard my cries for help.... I never ask for help. I never thought it would do any good." After sitting another minute or so like this, Emily's eyes became clearer. She looked directly at me and let her whole body relax into her chair. Then she recalled that she had never told her dad that she did not like going to the racetrack, that she would prefer they do something that was fun for her. And she realized that she almost never asked for love or connection from David. She had been unconsciously assuming she did not have the right to ask. Instead, she had developed a pattern of asking *him* how *he* was doing.

It soon became clear that Emily had spent her life protecting herself from being vulnerable to hearing no, from wanting something and not getting it. This issue was very painful in relationship to her dad, and now she was repeating it with her husband.

Doing this exercise just once helped Emily get in touch with all these feelings and insights. But her reluctance to ask for loving connection did not instantly disappear. Ultimately, she needed to repeat this practice many times, connecting with herself like this, holding space for her fearful parts. She needed to get familiar with the inner tension between the part of her that has wants and the part of her that fears asking. She needed to take time to get to know the little girl who got used to adapting to what her father wanted. In time, she learned to accept how vulnerable it feels to take emotional risks, how much it sometimes hurts to hear no or "not now," and how capable she is of bringing tenderness and connection to herself when no one else is available.

Developing Your Witnessing Self

In this book, when I invite you to pause and reflect on what you're reading, and to notice your sensations and feelings, this is intended to help you develop and deepen your capacity for self-observation. Human consciousness includes the objects of consciousness or awareness — the things you see, hear, sense, think, remember. Our consciousness can also be like a big open space in which these objects of consciousness occur. We could say that within consciousness, there is the witness, the thoughts or feelings being witnessed, and the space of presence.

The capacity to notice, to witness, or to self-observe is what Buddhist psychology calls *mindfulness*. In the Hindu chakra system, this is related to taking a "third-eye" perspective. The third eye is the energy center between the eyebrows. It sees everything from a spacious, all-accepting view — broader than the view of our everyday personality. Many other spiritual traditions also value this capacity for taking a bigger view. It is a way we humans have for getting "above the level of the problem."

Practicing Compassion for Your Inner Child is one method of becoming a witness to oneself, but it focuses on the past. Below, I provide a method for bringing mindful presence to trigger reactions as they are occurring. As children, many people come to believe that there's no room in this world for their emotional upsets, fears, or pain. Perhaps their parents got anxious, annoyed, or angry when they cried or fussed, so they developed the false belief: *If I am in pain, there's something wrong with me. I'm weak, defective, too sensitive, a nuisance, and I will be shunned, ignored, punished, or suppressed.* As adults, we sometimes continue the habit of judging or shaming ourselves when we are upset.

However, we can shed this faulty conditioning and become a wise and nurturing "holding environment" for all of our inner aspects. We can learn how to use our trigger reactions to reconnect with the parts of ourselves that have been abandoned — so we can heal the fear of emotional pain that causes us to reject parts of ourselves. The Compassionate Self-Inquiry practice below helps you get to know these buried or abandoned aspects and give them the loving attention they have always needed.

Exercise: Compassionate Self-Inquiry

The next step toward trigger mastery is learning how to work with a trigger reaction immediately after it occurs (or even while it is occurring). The Compassionate Self-Inquiry practice involves spending a little time *being with* the sensations, feelings, and fear-stories that have just been triggered. This involves noticing the various elements of your reactive experience (sensations, feelings, thoughts), and allowing these to be seen, felt, heard, or attended to. When you first begin practicing this, the whole process may take about fifteen minutes. Later on, it will take less time, until finally, you may be able to accomplish all the steps in less than one minute.

The Basic Practice

Immediately or soon after you experience a triggering event with another person, find a safe location in which you can be alone and uninterrupted for as long as you think you will need. This may not always be possible right away, but do it as soon as you can. If you have a pause agreement with someone, this is what you would do during the pause.

Once you are in a safe space, practice self-calming. Close your eyes, and take ten or more slow calming breaths through your nose. As you exhale, focus on relaxing the body and letting go of mental stories or attempts to figure anything out. Notice the sensations of the chair holding you. Feel where your body touches the chair. As you feel these sensations, continue with slow, conscious breathing. When you feel relaxed, note how this feels, and remember, you can always come back to this place whenever things get too intense — whether during this practice or in your life.

When you feel truly calm and safe, while still breathing fully and deeply, recall the triggering event: Where were you? Who was with you? What was said, done, or not done? Was there a gesture or a tone of voice that you reacted to? As you do this, take the viewpoint of the witness. Watch this event unfold before you with an attitude of openness, acceptance, and curiosity. If your mind starts to spin stories, explanations, or interpretations about the event, put these aside for now. At this point, you are building your inner capacity for recalling and witnessing feelings and sensations.

Next, consider your reaction in this triggering episode: What did you feel? What body sensations occurred? Did you do or say anything, or was your reaction mostly internal? Allow these feelings and sensations to come back. Let yourself feel these feelings, but this time, feel them with the support of your slow, conscious breathing, and with your inner witness available.

Sit with whatever feelings and sensations arise and let them be just as they are. Be interested or curious about them — as if these are aspects of yourself you wish to become more deeply acquainted with. As you observe your feelings, also notice this whole scene — notice your reactions to the triggering event as well as how it is to witness this. Is it difficult or painful? Does it feel supportive and nurturing to be with yourself in this way? Continue holding a nurturing, curious space for as long as you want or need, but don't be too quick to end the exercise. Your feelings or sensations may change quite a bit — in size, shape, location, temperature, weight — as you sit with them. Let this happen on its own. Let things move and change as they will. Doing this teaches you to trust your own process of working through difficult emotions. Every individual does this in their own unique way — for some, their inquiry process is like a straight line, moving quickly from here to there. For others, the route is more circuitous, moving more slowly or with more side excursions; see "Exploring Deeper Feelings and Memories" (pages 100–102). Then, when you feel ready, you can move to "Closing the Exercise" (pages 102–3).

Return to Self-Calming If You Feel Overwhelmed

If you ever start to feel overcome with the intensity of a feeling or memory, back off from this and return to your self-calming practice. Just notice the movement of your chest and belly as you breathe in and out. If you still feel overwhelmed or afraid, open your eyes and look around the room. Focus your attention on one object and describe its physical attributes (for example, "I see a green leather chair with little wheels on each of its four legs"). Then notice how you feel. If you feel calm and clear-minded, continue the exercise.

If not, take a break and do something else that feels nurturing — like listening to music or talking a walk. Another option is to get a blanket and wrap yourself in it as a way of giving comfort to yourself. Or just lie down with a blanket or a pillow. Try putting the palm of your hand directly on top of where your body sensations are, and feel the warmth of your palm radiating into your body. Rocking, hugging, patting, touching, and stroking yourself are all ways to show caring and nurturing toward yourself.

If you know you suffer from complex trauma or PTSD, be careful. If an old traumatic memory begins to overwhelm you, do whatever works for you to interrupt this memory — such as any of the things I suggest here. Even though this exercise focuses on recent, nontraumatic, interpersonal incidents, sometimes flashbacks can occur.

Exploring Deeper Feelings and Memories

As you recall and observe the triggering event, your thoughts might travel beyond the event itself. You might think about what led up to this event, why it should or should not have happened, what this means about your relationship with the other person, other feelings about yourself, any related events, and so on. Allow these thoughts and observe them; stay open and curious. Do your thoughts reveal a particular emotional attitude — like indignation, blame, shame, disappointment? Are there deeper, more vulnerable emotions underneath your thoughts — such as fears that no one cares, that you are alone, that you are not good enough, that your needs don't matter, and so on? Fears like these are often hidden under fairly reasonable-sounding thoughts. For example, Emily habitually said to herself, "Dad didn't know how to love." This strategy helped her avoid noticing fear about her own unworthiness.

When you notice one of your deeply protected or hidden fears coming up, this is a gift for further healing. If a vulnerable core fear comes to light, embrace this with tenderness. It may help to imagine that this fearful part of you is a much-loved child or a tender, vulnerable aspect of yourself. Be with yourself like this for a while, holding and comforting yourself, as you continue to breathe slowly and with awareness. Remember, a fear of something is a thought. A fear does not mean that the thought is true or real (like the fear of not being seen). Such fears point to ways in which some core developmental need was not adequately attended to (such as the need for loving attention).

Similarly, if you experience any reactive feelings like frustration, anger, shock, hopelessness, anxiety, or confusion, try to bring a compassionate attitude toward these feelings. As above, imagine that this upset part of you is a much-loved child or a tender aspect of yourself. Get to know this part and give it the love and understanding it has always needed. Encourage this hurting part to feel whatever arises. Allow feelings and sensations to move or change. If tears come, this can be helpful, as crying is a way the body moves stuck energy. Reassure this tender part that you are here, and you are willing to be here for as long as this takes. When you do this, you create a reassuring presence that makes space for your upset self to more fully feel the fears or insecurities that are beneath your triggers.

Old memories or familiar associations might also come up. You might get a familiar felt-sense that this adult trigger reaction is related to past experiences. An old memory might surface — from earlier in your adult life or from childhood. If a specific painful, scary, confusing, or upsetting childhood memory emerges, move your attention to that scene, and follow the Compassion for Your Inner Child exercise. While practicing self-calming, recall the old event; track your feelings, sensations, and thoughts; and allow space for the vulnerable fears to emerge. Hold whatever arises with an attitude of acceptance and curiosity. Be with yourself, allowing things inside of you to just be as they are and to change and move as they will.

Closing the Exercise

Whether or not other feelings or earlier memories surface, allow yourself to feel whatever comes up. You might even have things you wish to express out loud. Let yourself speak, shout, or cry if you are moved to. Imagine speaking to the other person involved in the triggering incident, saying out loud whatever words come to you. If you feel moved to, speak soothing words to your tender, vulnerable self (or to your inner child or the younger you). Let your words be nurturing and empathetic. For example, say things like "Wow, that was intense. You showed a lot of courage to let yourself go there," or "I love you. I'm here for you." If no words come, that's fine, too. Expressing yourself with words is not essential to your healing.

When you feel ready — after you have felt your feelings for longer than you ordinarily would, explored any deeper emotions or memories that arise, and nurtured yourself through these feelings — then you can bring this to a close. Find a comfortable, restful position for your body, and take about ten slow, calming breaths. Open your eyes and begin to move your body — but only when you feel like it. Get up slowly. Be gentle with yourself, and don't hurry. Walk around a bit, sensing your body as you walk. Notice if you are more aware of your sensations. Continue to be aware of your breath as you gradually reenter your normal life activities. Give yourself appreciation for allowing yourself to experience what you have just experienced.

The Good Mother Archetype

The essential goal of these practices is to learn to feel painful or uncomfortable feelings and sensations while also compassionately witnessing them. It's like the bigger you is feeling empathy for a vulnerable, tender, or younger part of you. In the Compassion for Your Inner Child exercise, as you review what happened to this tender part of you, you may have seen why the event in question was so upsetting or scary to the younger you. If you felt empathy, your tender self now has a lot more support than it once had. You are developing a new, more supportive relationship with yourself. You are activating your inner good parent, your good mother archetype, your inner protector.

Everyone has inside of their psyche the template for being a good parent. Everyone knows what feels good, beneficial, healthy, loving, and what does not. It's true that your ability to easily access this inner good parent may have been eclipsed by unfortunate childhood experiences, but I assure you, the good parent or good mother archetype is part of every human's potential. Sometimes, we first need to activate the intent to uncover this hidden resource.

Resistance Is Part of the Process

In doing these practices, you might notice a tendency to shut down before really feeling everything. For instance, you might find yourself analyzing why something happened rather than just feeling what happened. This sort of resistance to uncomfortable feelings is a normal part of the process. It could be something you learned to do back in childhood to protect yourself. You learned to abort the process of experiencing feelings by going into your head instead. Just go as far as you can with this exercise, encouraging the hurting or upset part of yourself to feel and express your hurt, knowing that the adult you is witnessing this with acceptance and compassion. It is actually better to do these practices in small doses rather than trying to keep going deeper in one sitting.

In particular, do the Compassionate Self-Inquiry exercise again and again — with the same or different triggering incidents. It takes many repetitions to unlearn conditioned habits for avoiding emotional discomfort. Life gives us the opportunity to revisit our core fears again and again, until we have fully felt in a conscious, self-loving way everything we have left to feel.

Some people ask what to do if they have a judgmental or contemptuous attitude toward their triggered self. What if you don't like the wounded part of yourself? What if you view this part as evidence that you are unlovable? What if you think you should be more together or should be over it by now? If this happens for you, notice this, and notice what you feel about this. How do you feel about the fact that you get impatient with yourself? If a child was crying in fear or pain, and a parent told the child to grow up or get over it, what might you feel? Is your relationship to yourself similar to this impatient parent? Notice how you feel about how you treat yourself. If you feel sadness, this is probably a good start. This may be the beginning of a softer, more empathetic attitude toward the vulnerable or triggered parts of yourself.

Keep Practicing Being with Sensations and Emotions

Do not expect to get over your trigger reactions right away. Some may never go away completely. But if you do this practice regularly, you will not be so quick to become reactive. All the *pausing* and *being with* that you are doing will help you slow down your automatic reactions, allowing you time to bring more awareness and insight to whatever is happening. At first, just accept that your core feelings and needs will be hidden from view when you experience a trigger reaction, and that you will have a tendency to react from fear rather than acting from conscious choice. Learn to pause and self-calm as soon as you notice reactivity. During your pause, practice Compassionate Self-Inquiry. This is preparation for doing the repair process (see chapter 6), or if repair is not indicated or appropriate, it is preparation for getting back to being your best, most resourceful self.

Even if you do the Compassionate Self-Inquiry practice hours or even days after an incident, it will work. Every time you do it, you are taking a step toward healing old hurts and completing your past, allowing long-suppressed feelings and sensations to move and be metabolized. In the past, you may have had to shut down painful or fearful feelings because it wasn't safe or you didn't have enough support. So they never got to resolve themselves through the natural healing-by-feeling process. Now you have more inner resources to bring to the matter. You are learning to create a safe container for your core needs to be felt and attended to. Now your stuck feelings and unmet needs for love and safety have room to move. In time, as you learn to be with uncomfortable feelings, you will be able to more easily allow upset feelings to change and transform inside you.

When we can openly admit we get triggered sometimes, we won't feel the need to hide our weaknesses. We become less defensive, which is always a good thing. We won't be afraid of being found out or of looking bad if we're not perfectly together. Having nothing to hide is a great boon to self-trust and feeling safe in the world. This opens us up to creating the kind of loving partnerships and friendships where we do these practices with others, which helps everyone heal childhood wounds and rewire insecure brain circuits.

Chapter Six

Repairing and Clearing the Air

Restoring Connection with Others

As you come to know each other's sensitivities, this helps you get over the tendency to take the other person's reactive behavior personally.

Repair is the final step in the Five Steps of Trigger Work program. This is where we come back to the other person (or persons, if the situation involves a group) and ask for a do-over or share our genuine sorrow for how our behavior impacted them. This is also where we would reveal the vulnerable fears and fear-stories that were at the root of our trigger reaction and get some reassurance that our fear-story is not true.

Note that the repair step is not necessary if we are triggered on our own or while alone, such as when something we read or see in a film restimulates old wounds. Our work is complete once we have done the Compassionate Self-Inquiry practice in step four. However, most attachment triggers occur while interacting with others, and so the process is not over until step five is complete.

Repairing is used after an interaction where one or both people went into a fight, flight, or freeze state and acted from that state in a way that disrupted feelings of safety, connection, or trust. It should also be used when one person's reactivity is not obvious to the other person — where one person got triggered, did not reveal this, but later wants to come clean. Sometimes a unilateral repair is necessary — which is actually somewhat of a confession, as in: "You didn't know this, but when you said you wanted to skip dinner, I got triggered. My fear-of-rejection button got pushed. I had the story that you're pulling away from me ... and now I think I need some reassurance that we're okay."

Doing the Compassionate Self-Inquiry practice just prior to any repair will help the repair process go more smoothly. Each time you do this self-inquiry, you are helping yourself take in stride what I like to call "the normal pains of an adult relationship." As you learn to accept and soothe your pain, this lessens the need to blame the other person because you are learning to have a new relationship to yourself when you are hurting or upset. As acceptance increases over time, you more easily relate to a trigger reaction as something familiar: *Ah, I know this place. It's one of my core fears. I can hold this pain tenderly. No one is to blame.* The ability to let go of blame is essential to repair, since blaming is a reaction to being triggered. If you are still blaming, you are not yet ready to repair and should repeat the Compassionate Self-Inquiry practice.

As part of your repair process, it can be powerful to share with your partner what you discover about yourself during your self-inquiry. This helps your partner know you more deeply and have empathy for your fears or sensitivities. As you come to know each other's sensitivities, this helps you get over the tendency to take the other person's reactive behavior personally.

The repair step is not appropriate in some types of relationships because the repair practice described here is usually done by prior mutual agreement. Some business relationships, for example, do not lend themselves to this sort of up-front agreement, but it is still good to apologize or offer a verbal do-over. In an intimate relationship, especially one where partners get into frequent reactive cycles, this step is vital. It is also vital for parents to know how to repair a rift in connection with their child. When a parent gets triggered by a child's behavior, the fact of being triggered means the parent momentarily goes into their own self-oriented fear reaction. When a parent is angry, upset, or otherwise in reactivity, this is scary for the child, who will likely feel cut off from the parent's love. So, parents need to be able to go back to their child after this type of triggering incident to reestablish a loving connection (see chapter 8 for more on this).

Why Repair?

Most intimate partners recognize the need to make up after a fight. In other types of relationships, people may try to "get over it" without saying much. In this book, I encourage you to use these practices no matter what your relationship status. By developing these skills, we can reduce the amount of unfinished business with people in our life, and perhaps avoid having friendships, partnerships, or dating relationships end abruptly without our understanding why.

The usual way most people try to repair does not work. Their attempts involve too many words, too much explanation, too much trying to be heard. Instead of repair, what occurs is more like a rehash, except with calmer voices. After a typical long-winded repair, people end up feeling just as unsafe or unheard as before. One sign that a repair is not working is when people start repeating themselves. If this happens, it means they are still triggered or have gotten retriggered.

The repair practice here is simple and short. It focuses on speaking from your heart to the other person's emotional center, to the part of the brain where their survival alarm system is located. You speak directly to what feels unsafe or afraid in the other person. Reasonable-sounding but long-winded explanations can cause the brain's emotional centers to shut down, since they send the message that someone is more interested in clearing their good name than in being present to the other person's feelings. It takes fewer words to speak the emotional truth.

This book's repair practice is based on the idea that no one is to blame for anyone else's emotional sensitivities. Once we accept that we are not to blame for the other person's reactions, we can let go of the need to defend ourselves. This opens the way to feel genuine sorrow and caring for the other person. During repair, both people reveal the (possible) early origins of their sensitivities. This helps people feel empathy for each other. With such vulnerable revelations, the tendency to blame or feel blamed dissolves. The repair practice also includes a way to safely request reassurance that our fears are unfounded and to offer any reassurances that the other might need. This type of exchange restores a sense of safety between people and can even help them rewire the insecure brain circuits that have been with them since childhood.

Deciding Whether You Are Ready to Repair

One of the biggest problems that I see in couple relationships is how difficult it is for partners to tolerate their partner being unhappy with them. Many people find it very hard to take time to pause and self-soothe before trying to talk things out. So they keep talking (or reacting) when they ought to be pausing. One of my main goals in this book is to give people tools that help them tolerate the uncomfortable time period between getting triggered and repairing. These tools will give you the confidence that the process of getting triggered and repairing, of disconnection and reconnection, follows a predictable, orderly sequence of events that you can learn. It takes inner work and a measure of self-discipline, but most people can learn these tools.

When someone cannot stand the anxiety of any sort of separation, they often try to repair trigger reactivity before they are really ready. Maybe they'll do a perfunctory pause, but they don't really take the time to get themselves feeling calm and safe. They may try to soothe their hurting or wounded self, but their mind keeps going somewhere else. One sign of not being ready is noticing, during your pause, that you are having the same upsetting thoughts about the other person over and over. This does not help, but for some people, it's a habit that's hard to break.

Another clue that someone is trying to repair too soon is when they don't yet feel at least some measure of generosity or friendliness toward their partner. They may still be holding the other person to an unrealistically high standard for how that person should have behaved — failing to recognize that the other person was triggered, that this was not their best self, and that their actions or words didn't reflect their true feelings.

Another clue is when someone replays their fear-story (or blaming story) in their mind. They might even want their partner to validate their story as part of the repair, saying things like "You *were* flirting with that woman ... admit it." If you have already identified this sort of suspiciousness as part of your trigger signature, get in the habit of questioning your suspicious thoughts before acting on them.

With all that said, if you start your repair before both of you are ready, it's not the end of the world. Hopefully, you will realize this as soon as you see yourselves going around in circles getting nowhere, and you'll call for another pause. If this happens, take more time to self-calm and self-soothe. Also, it sometimes occurs that people get retriggered all over again while trying to repair — even if they started out calm. If someone gets retriggered during the repair, just ask for another pause, calm yourselves, and wait a while before trying again.

You're Ready for Repair When ...

Do not try to repair until these things are true:

- During your pause, you did some breath and body awareness practices to get calm and to remind yourself that there is no real danger.
- You realized you have felt these feelings before, and you will probably feel them again.
- You recognized your reactive stories as part of your trigger signature.
- If you got triggered in a close friendship, family relationship, or intimate partnership, you realized that you two have probably experienced something like this before, and eventually, you got through it.
- During your self-inquiry, you connected with your

present upset feelings and hung out with these long enough to discover whether they were connected to any earlier painful memories. If so, you made note of any past unmet needs or childhood wounds.

- Whatever you discovered, you took time to be with your tender, wounded, or sensitive self with empathy and compassion.
- You gave yourself caring and reassurance of safety.

Now you are ready to fill out your repair statement in preparation for meeting with the other person to do your repair. Your repair process will go much more smoothly if you have done these steps to help you fully take responsibility for your own trigger reaction and accept yourself, warts and all.

Cotriggering Lite and Cotriggering Dark

Different situations require different types and levels of repair — depending on how triggered both people were and how long reactivity was allowed to play out. Then there is the situation where only one person was triggered. This person's reaction was not obvious to the other, but there was a rupture in this person's feelings of safety and trust that affected the relationship. First I'll address *cotriggering*, which is when both people are triggered. Cotriggering occurs when the two parties are so emotionally connected that when one person becomes triggered, the other person also feels unsafe, and so they react with their own trigger signature behavior.

Some cotriggering behaviors can threaten the relationship deeply, even to the point of traumatizing or retraumatizing someone. Other reactions are less threatening, and thus easier to repair. I have coined the terms *cotriggering dark* and *cotriggering lite* to refer to those different reactive behaviors, distinguishing those that cut deep and those that are less threatening.

Cotriggering dark means that when two people react in a triggered way, at least one person's behavior includes one or more of these elements: It is extremely aggressive, including yelling, name-calling, physical violence, punching something, having a tantrum, or threatening to end the relationship; it is extremely demeaning, such as using labels like wimp, narcissist, bitch, pervert, or idiot for the other person; or it is extremely cold, such as pretending not to hear the other, acting as if the other does not exist, and so on.

Cotriggering lite means two people react with triggered behavior, but they both express being upset in milder ways. They may show anger, disappointment, frustration, defensiveness, or mistrust. They might blame or use judgmental labels, but they do not use threatening postures — like getting in someone's face — demeaning words, or loud voices. Here are some of the most common cotriggering lite reactions: asking a lot of questions, being suspicious, being protective or defensive, holding unrealistic expectations, holding judgmental or blaming thoughts, explaining, insisting you are right, insisting that the other validate your story, debating, repeating yourself, or freezing up.

Whether an episode was experienced as dark or lite will determine how many times the same incident needs to be repaired. Most cotriggering lite situations can be repaired in one repair session. But cotriggering dark situations, when one or both parties engage in extreme aggression and demeaning or dismissive language, might require doing the various aspects of repair quite a few times.

For some individuals, almost anything that results in their feeling not approved of or not validated can cut deep. Other people who are more secure and confident will recover more easily. So *lite* and *dark* are relative terms. Harsher behavior toward a more sensitive partner is likely to require several repair sessions.

Lying is a unique case — I do not consider this a "lite" situation, even though there is no aggression or demeaning involved. If one or both partners lie, this qualifies as cotriggering dark, and it may also require numerous apologies, repairs, and even amends.

Preparing Your Repair Statement after Cotriggering

The time between your *pause* and your *repair* might be short (ten to fifteen minutes), medium (one to three hours), or long (three to eight hours). As soon as you can, after doing your Compassionate Self-Inquiry, sit down with a copy of the repair statement and fill in the blanks, as shown below ("The Repair Statement"). Doing this right after your inner inquiry increases the likelihood that you will be in a tender, forgiving frame of mind as you prepare for repair.

Filling out the repair statement is like a journaling exercise. You sit with yourself and reflect on what happened, what you felt and thought, how you reacted, where this reaction came from, and what you need now in order to restore a sense of safety or connection. Each time you do a repair, you become more accepting of the fact that trigger reactions happen to everyone, and they happen to you. With practice, you will find it easier to admit your fears and insecurities. This will make it easier to recognize these insecurities the moment they are arising. Instead of acting out fears in a triggered way, you gradually learn to spot and reveal fears right away, and then to ask for the help or reassurance you need — without repeating over and over the painful cycle of reactivity followed by repair.

During a repair, both persons will fill out the statement shown below. Then you meet at the agreed-upon time and ask each other, "Is this a good time to do our repair, or does one of us need more time?" When you both agree that you are calm, self-soothed, and ready, you take turns reading your statements out loud, reading slowly while pausing to look into the other person's eyes. After each person's turn delivering their repair statement, the other person should offer a brief reassuring response that speaks to the other's core need. For a template of this response, see "The Reassuring Response" (pages 119–20).

The Repair Statement

Here is the repair statement template, which you complete separately every time you repair. In the blank spaces, fill in the specifics of what happened, what you understand, and how you feel per the instructions in brackets.

> **I now see that when I** _____ [insert your reactive behavior in specific or general terms, such as: *said, "Get over it" or "You're manipulating me," got defensive, walked out, took offense*], **I was triggered**.
>
> **That was probably my fear of** _____ [insert your core fear, such as: *not being seen or valued, being blamed or criticized, abandonment, not being good enough*] **coming up**.
>
> **When I heard [or saw] you** _____ [insert the other person's words or behavior, such as: *heard you say, "Stop manipulating me," or heard you raise your voice*, or *saw you pause and look away*], **the story I told myself was** _____ [insert your reactive story, such as: *my needs don't matter, I'm not good enough, I'm being rejected, I'm not accepted as I am*].

Optional: This triggered feelings similar to when _____ [insert childhood memory, such as: *my dad would promise things and not come through* or *no one listened to me at the dinner table*].

I'm sorry I _____ [insert your reactive behavior, the same one named above].

I can see how that would _____ [insert the other person's reaction, such as: *trigger, upset, hurt,* or *frighten*] **you.**

Optional: I also want to say _____ [add a further apology or explanation, such as: *you didn't deserve that, I didn't mean that,* or *I don't really think that*].

If I could do it over, I would have said that my fear of _____ [insert your core fear, the same one named above] **was triggered and that I needed your help to feel** _____ [insert your core need, such as: *accepted, good enough, loved by you, that my needs matter, that my voice matters, that I'm not to blame*].

As an example of how these statements might read, here are two that were written and shared by a married couple, Dilraj and Denise, when they did a repair. First, here is Denise's repair statement:

Dilraj, I'd like to repair what just happened. I see now that when I said, "Why do I bother trying?!" I was triggered. That was my old fear that I'm not important coming up. When I heard you say you wouldn't be home till ten, the story my mind made up was, "His work is more important than our marriage. I'm not important to him anymore." This triggered feelings similar to when my father left our family and never came back. I'm sorry I said that and then pulled away. I can see how that would hurt you. If I could do it over, and was calm enough, I would have said, "I'm getting triggered. It's my old fear of not feeling important, that I don't matter." I need your help feeling I am important to you, that I do matter.

Here is Dilraj's repair statement:

Denise, I'd like to repair what happened when I said, "What's wrong now?" I see now that when I said that, I was triggered. That was my old fear that I'm not enough coming up. When I heard you say something about why do you bother, the story my mind made up was, "She's criticizing me. I've done something wrong again. Maybe I'm flawed or there's something wrong with me." This triggered feelings similar to when my mother was sick for all those years, and I kept getting told I was making too much noise and making her sicker. I'm sorry I said that. I can see how that would hurt you. If I could do it over and was calm enough, I would have said, "I'm getting triggered. It's my old fear of not being good enough, or of feeling flawed or bad." I need your help to feel I am good enough.

In both of these repair statements, we see the following important elements:

1. Dilraj and Denise both owned that they got triggered and named their reactive behavior.
2. They revealed their core fears.
3. They revealed something about the childhood origins of their insecurities.

4. They apologized.
5. They revised what they originally said to practice a more responsible way of speaking.
6. They asked for reassurance or help using noncontrolling language.

In the last item, *noncontrolling language* refers to making a request (or expressing a need) versus telling the other person what they should do. Controlling language, which I *don't* recommend, would be: "I need you to make me more of a priority." Noncontrolling language, which I *do* recommend, would be: "I need your help feeling like a priority," or "I need to feel like I'm a priority."

The Reassuring Response

After one person listens intently to their partner's repair statement, that person should give a reassuring response. This is a simple statement of understanding and love that is preferably accompanied by gentle touch, eye contact, and a soothing voice. Here are some examples:

I do love you... very much.

I love you just as you are.

I really do respect you.

I do accept you just as you are.

You are good enough, more than good enough.

I would never abandon you. I'm in this for the long haul.

I do value spending time with you. I want you to know this.

Your needs are so very important to me.

I want to know and hear your needs and feelings.
I want you to feel safe with me and know that I do not
blame you.

In essence, every repair statement is meant to end with the person expressing what reassurance they need (to feel loved, accepted, and so on). Ideally, the reassuring response would be a sincere statement that directly addresses that need. If you are not feeling spacious and friendly enough to do this, then find something you appreciate and offer that, such as, "I appreciate you for letting me know how you feel." Or just offer a hug.

Sometimes it helps to use a preamble, such as: "I see your need now, and I want to give you that. I want to give you what I couldn't last night. I do want to hear your needs." That said, watch out for and avoid a challenging, demeaning, or defensive preamble, such as: "Of course…" (as in, "Of course, your needs matter!"), "You should know by now…," "How many times have I told you…," or "Don't be silly.…" These phrases are generally not reassuring.

Repairing "Bad Timing" or Not Pausing Soon Enough

Finally, as I note in chapter 4, it's very common at first for people to fail to pause soon enough, that is, at the first sign of being triggered. If this happens, I recommend that you address this during your repair. After two people have shared their repair statements and offered reassuring responses, I recommend that one or both persons acknowledge that it would have been smart to initiate the pause sooner, and then to specifically name the point when they wished they had paused. This way, in addition to repairing your trigger reactions, you also repair your "bad timing" — the fact that you waited too long to pause or perhaps talked over your partner's request to pause.

Here is an example of a "bad timing" repair statement:

I see now that I should have said "pause" when
_____ [insert your triggered behavior, such as: *I raised my voice, I started feeling angry*, and so on].

If I could do it over, I would _____ [insert the correct behavior, such as: *say "pause" at that moment*, or *stop talking when you said "pause"*].

I'm sorry I didn't say "pause" sooner.

Unilateral Repair:
When Only One Person Is Triggered

There are situations in relationships where one person gets triggered and has their own private reactive behavior, reactive fear, and reactive story, and all the while the other person has no idea this is happening. In fact, the triggered person might not even realize they were triggered until hours later. When this happens, I recommend doing a unilateral repair, in which the person who was triggered acknowledges and apologizes for their behavior. Many people are tempted to skip this. After all, if the other person doesn't know and wasn't triggered, why does the *relationship* need repair? However, when two people are in an ongoing relationship that values honesty and intimacy, this type of vulnerable self-disclosure helps people deepen trust, intimacy, and self-compassion.

In addition, if someone decides not to mention that they were triggered, there is the danger that they may not really let go of their reactive story about their partner. Remember, our story is the meaning we give to triggered behavior based on our own insecurities. In my experience, this is what tends to happen when triggers do not get cleared. Reactive stories reside in our long-term memory as a sort of magnet for other similar incidents. These build and grow if they remain unaddressed. And if we begin to believe our fear-based stories about our partner, we may even adapt our behavior to fit our distorted view. Then, one day, when we get into a bigger disagreement with our partner, and we are both triggered, all the fear-stories that have been stored up can come pouring out in a barrage. This is the reason unilateral repairs are important, since they help people avoid the buildup of negative stories about each other.

Here is a hypothetical example of a married couple, Molly and Barry. Molly wishes Barry would spend more quality time with her. On one particular day, Barry informs her he has to attend a work-related seminar that upcoming weekend. Molly feels hurt and disappointed. The fear-story that plays in her mind is: "He looks for excuses to get away from me." Her childhood fear of abandonment is triggered, and she remembers once being left at home with a babysitter while her parents took her other siblings on a family vacation. Molly says nothing in the moment, but an hour later, she approaches Barry and says, "You're always so busy. Maybe you need to take a time-management course." Barry grunts something that sounds like agreement, and nothing more is said about this. Then, the next day, Molly notices a vague feeling of discomfort and recurring fearful thoughts about whether Barry is capable of sustaining a long-term intimate relationship. Since Molly already knows that "fantasizing leaving" is part of her trigger signature, she now recognizes that she was triggered the previous day but tried to hide it and instead mentioned something about a time-management course. Here's how she clears the air and repairs this feeling of distance and disconnection.

First, on her own, she fills out a unilateral repair statement (see below). Then she lets Barry know she wants to talk, saying, "I have some feelings to clear from something that happened yesterday. Is this a good time?" If he says yes, she reads her statement.

The Unilateral Repair Statement

When I heard (or saw) you _____ [insert triggering words or actions, such as: *heard you say, "I'm going to that seminar this weekend"*], **I got triggered.**

It was probably my old fear of _____ [insert your core fear, such as: *abandonment*] **coming up.**

You didn't realize this was happening, but I want to come clean, so I can let it go and feel closer [or *more trusting, more connected,* and so on] **with you.**

Optional: The story I told myself was _____ [insert your reactive story, such as: *"I'm not wanted. He doesn't like being with me"*].

Optional: This triggered feelings similar to when _____ [insert childhood memory, such as: *when my parents and siblings went on vacation and left me at home*].

I'm sorry I _____ [insert reactive or automatic behavior, such as: *didn't tell you, gave you that phony smile, made that controlling remark about taking a time-management course*].

Optional: That was my control pattern [or *I was on automatic,* or *I was not aware of my real feelings until later*].

If I could do it over, I would tell you that my fear of _____ [insert your core fear, the same one named above] **was triggered**.

I also would have told you I need your help _____ [insert your core need, such as: *to feel that I am wanted and loved*].

Stick to the Script

When people first learn to repair, they can find it difficult to stick to the repair script. They may think the wording feels unnatural or insincere. They may be tempted to improvise. I urge you to write out your repair statement and deliver it exactly as it is written. When you don't do this, there is a strong likelihood that you will wind up using too many words or slipping into old unconscious communication habits — like explaining.

Even if you do stick to the script, however, one of you might get retriggered somewhere in the process. If this happens, you will need to pause, self-calm, and self-soothe again. It is not unusual for retriggering to happen during repair or reassurance — especially when people are first learning the repair practice. The words might sound stiff or too scripted and therefore seem insincere. People may resist speaking so carefully. These practices are designed to feel unnatural — because our "natural" communication habits are often what trigger others. Cut yourself and your partner some slack and recognize there is a learning curve. It is not easy to go against your natural tendencies. Try not to get discouraged. And be gentle with yourself.

Part Two

Applying the Practices in Relationships

Chapter Seven

I'm Triggered with My Intimate Partner

The phenomenon of cotriggering presents a serious dilemma for many couples. Just when your partner needs you the most, that is when you are the least emotionally present.

Triggers, or the reactive behaviors and stories that arise around triggers, are the biggest impediment to trust and respect that most couples will face. But when you know how to work with your reactivity and repair quickly, this is the best way to deepen trust and respect. So the sickness becomes the cure. Part 1 of this book outlines the basics of how to work with your triggers. This chapter covers some of the issues that apply specifically to couples.

Relationship as a Practice

An intimate partnership is a breeding ground for triggers. Because of this, it is also the best context for healing childhood wounds or trauma and for transcending childhood conditioning. I suggest viewing the relationship as a practice. This means that, as in practices like yoga or meditation, you *expect* to encounter discomfort. You know effort and self-discipline are required. Rather than respond with dismay or shock, you welcome unexpected challenges for what they can teach you about yourself. Also like yoga and meditation, you know experienced teachers can show you where to put your efforts so they bear the most fruit. This chapter will show you how to maximize your learning and sustain your efforts — so your relationship feels like a safe haven rather than a chore.

Failures and setbacks are part of any learning process. So are successes and rewards. Since there is always the risk that efforts may not pay off, you should ask yourself: Are you willing to embark on this journey of mutual self-discovery with this person, not knowing if you will succeed or where it might lead? Are you willing to share your fears and insecurities, your weaknesses and deficits, your deepest desires, your selfish wants, your secrets? This journey is not for everyone. You may not be sure yet if it is for you. Your answer will become clear as you progress along this path. You can quit anytime. But even if *intimate partnership as a practice* is not your path, it is still nice to have better communication skills.

The primary lesson in this relationship school is learning to work with your triggers in a cooperative way. In a partnership, it is both partners' responsibility to help create an atmosphere of safety, trust, healing, honesty, fairness, and respect for differences.

Cotriggering: We Are Wired Together

Every couple operates as a biological "herd of two." In the animal kingdom, members of a herd depend on one another for survival, so they instinctively react when any member of the herd seems to be in danger. In a herd, each member's interests are best served when the whole herd is healthy and safe. In a herd of gazelles, for example, if one gazelle senses danger and is triggered to run (choosing flight in the fight-flight-freeze response), the whole herd will get cotriggered and start running in the same direction. Likewise, in a human herd of two, if one partner gets triggered, this will disrupt the other's sense of safety. Neither may be aware of this subtle disturbance in connection, but it affects them nonetheless. How one person reacts will affect their partner.

So remember this lesson: When your partner gets triggered, you are very likely to become triggered also — even if you don't exhibit your reaction in an obvious way. Don't expect yourself to be too great at holding a safe space for a triggered partner — because you yourself might also feel unsafe. This works both ways. If you are triggered, don't expect your partner to always be able to hold a safe space or listen in the way you want when you're angry or upset. Very few partners are able to hold a neutral or loving space for an angry partner. Both partners need to maintain realistic expectations and know that, most of the time, if one person gets triggered, the other will become cotriggered. Each person's survival alarm will start ringing; their nervous system will activate into fight, flight, or freeze; and their options will narrow. Many times, being "wired together" is a good thing because it reinforces a sense of connection. But when partners get triggered, it means they're not much help to each other.

The phenomenon of cotriggering presents a serious dilemma for many couples. Just when your partner needs you the most, that is when you are the least emotionally present. This can restimulate childhood memories of being in distress and feeling as if you are all alone. But if you both know about cotriggering, your expectations will be more realistic. You'll see this as normal. This helps you recognize that you both need to pause and bring more mindfulness to the situation as soon as you can. That's why you need to be well-practiced in the pause-calm-repair sequence. These practices help you slow things down so you can pay better attention, see more of the whole picture, and address root causes. When you get good at using these practices, you will more easily recognize when you are entering tender or dangerous territory.

Exercise: Communicating About Your Trigger Signatures

Knowing your own and your partner's trigger signatures is a big part of this. It helps you take your trigger reactions in stride — because you accept (and even expect) that triggering will happen. Here is an exercise to help you communicate more easily about your trigger signatures. It is an exercise for you and your partner to do together, sitting side by side or facing each other. Set aside about an hour when you will not be interrupted.

To begin, both of you should pay attention to how relaxed and safe you feel in the moment. If either of you do not feel completely relaxed and safe, both of you should close your eyes and sit quietly while attending to your body sensations and breathing. Do this for a few minutes, feeling yourself letting go and relaxing a little more each time you exhale.

As you do this, notice if a disturbing thought, feeling, or memory comes to mind. If one does, see if you can expand your breathing. As you inhale, imagine you are becoming bigger or more spacious to make space for this inner disturbance. See if you can allow the disturbance to be there as you embrace it with the open presence of your attention. From this attitude of openness, of spacious allowing, see if you can view this disturbance as a part of yourself that needs love. From this place of acceptance, notice the sensations and feelings of this hurt or upset part. Embrace these feelings with your open, loving presence. Continue to breathe fully in order to support any increased excitement or anxiety. Be with yourself this way for a minute or two. You may have the impulse to give yourself a warm hug or to place one or both of your hands somewhere on your body as a gesture of reassurance or soothing. Try this, if it feels right.

Only continue with the exercise once both of you feel safe and relaxed. If that doesn't feel possible, then try again at a different time.

Recalling a Triggering Episode

When you are both ready to engage in a conversation, recall a recent but not too intense triggering episode. Choose an incident that you both remember. Then, each of you should reflect on the incident silently, in your own mind, and then separately fill in the blanks in this worksheet:

I got triggered when _____ [insert what you actually heard, saw, or thought].

When that happened, I felt _____ [insert your reactive feeling, such as: *anger, fear, confusion*].

When that happened, my body sensations were _____ [insert your reactive body sensations, such as: *a tense belly, heat in my face*].

When that happened, the fear-story my mind made up was _____ [insert your reactive stories or thoughts, such as: *"I don't matter," "I'm being rejected"*].

And I reacted by _____ [insert your reactive behaviors, such as: *arguing, explaining, walking out, having judgmental thoughts*].

After filling in this worksheet, you and your partner read your responses to each other and then discuss each person's typical trigger signature. This requires listening openly and without judgment, so that neither person is retriggered (see the next section). Remember, the goal of this exercise is to get better at noticing and naming the various elements of each partner's trigger signature. You are not going back over the incident to resolve it.

As you speak, notice if you are able to read your answers as written. Do you find yourself adding explanations, justifications, blaming remarks, apologies, or other extra data? If you add extra information, be self-aware and self-reflective about this. What is your aim in doing so? Do you have a habit of adding more information than necessary when you communicate? Is this an attempt to look good, seem knowledgeable, be right, protect yourself, manage uncertainty, or feel in control?

Or have you added comments because you never felt heard or understood regarding this incident, and you want to be heard now. If this is the case, it is a sign you are still triggered about the incident and probably unable to objectively witness what happened. When either person recognizes this is happening, pause the discussion and practice self-calming. Be with your feelings and sensations in a nurturing way until you feel calm and relaxed. Then return to the discussion and resume where you left off. Or, if necessary, set aside a time later to come back and do a repair together, where you get to acknowledge your need for reassurance that your needs matter or have been heard.

Listening Openly and Without Judgment to Avoid Retriggering

As you and your partner listen to each other, the intention is to understand and remember what the other describes about their trigger reactions. The goal is for you both to know and recognize each other's trigger signature. To do this well, you both need to feel safe and trust that the other person is taking responsibility for getting triggered in this way. Aim to view your partner's disclosures as an effort to be more accepting and aware about triggers — not as an indictment of you.

If you notice yourself feeling judgmental or resistant to something you hear, make note of this. Maybe your partner has a blind spot about this trigger reaction. Maybe during the incident in question, your partner got out of control or said something hurtful and is now forgetting to mention this. If there is a significant discrepancy between how your partner remembers the reaction and how you remember it, ask if you can share your recollections and offer some tentative edits to your partner's worksheet. But do not do this or even open up the topic unless you are feeling relaxed and friendly toward your partner. It is entirely possible to feel friendly and still disagree. Couples need practice with this, so this exercise can be good practice for learning to have a friendly feeling between the two of you as you discuss a difference in views.

The thing that leads to unfriendliness is the need to be right or the need to always have your views validated. Some people get triggered by any difference or disagreement. If one of you is especially sensitive to "not being validated," then you will need to bring a great deal of mindfulness to any discussion of your differences. Be aware that if you or your partner has this sort of sensitivity, then you both may experience frequent retriggering and cotriggering. It goes with the territory of having such insecurities. So during this exercise, it's best to be prepared to pause, self-calm, and self-soothe fairly often. Don't try to push through the exercise if either of you gets retriggered. You cannot bypass reactivity. Get used to going back into your silent pause, calming your nervous system, and starting over.

Debriefing the Exercise and Further Practice

Once you both feel finished with the conversation about your trigger signatures, take a moment to reflect with your partner on the conversation itself. Was it easier to identify one person's trigger signature and not so easy to see the other person's? In retrospect, do you recognize subtle signs of triggering in both partners that neither of you were aware of at the time? Be sure to look together at how difficult it can be to know for sure who got triggered first. And discuss any evidence that supports the theory that when one person gets triggered, this affects how calm and safe the other person feels.

When cotriggering occurs, this can leave partners feeling all alone to deal with their upset feelings. But if we know this and are actively cooperating in an effort to catch and halt triggers right away by learning each other's trigger signature, then we will not feel so alone. Doing this exercise together will help you feel like a team, where your mutual aim is to catch and halt reactivity and to get both of you feeling calm and safe before trying to repair.

Keep repeating this exercise as you both work at developing your trigger mastery skills. After a while, you will become familiar enough with both of your trigger signatures so that you'll be able to call for a pause before things escalate. This is your goal. We can't stop reactivity, but we can improve how we handle it, particularly as both partners become deeply engaged in their own inner work. Doing the inner work means doing these practices over and over and over. Inner work promotes the uncovering of lost or rejected parts of yourself, compassionately accepting these parts, and integrating these lost parts into your wholeness. Once integrated, these formerly lost parts come into a new relationship with the more beneficial aspects of yourself. You are developing a more intimate, loving, and trusting relationship with yourself. The aim is to include everything, not to get rid of anything. Thinking you are supposed to get over being triggered will impede this inner work. Instead, as you become more whole, you will gradually feel less reactive and more able to take hurts and disappointments in stride.

Your Reactive Cycle

If you study your triggering episodes for a while, you will probably notice a pattern or cycle. As in: The more one person questions, the more the other hides, and the more the other hides, the more the first person questions. Or the more one person criticizes, the more the other defends, and vice versa. When partners are cotriggered, it can seem like they are caught in a vicious cycle. It's not clear how they got there or who started it. They seem to be having the same fight as last time and the time before that. Even if the subject matter is different, it's always the same fight. In a way, it is, since the same core fears are getting triggered and the same core needs are trying to get met. This familiar repetitive cycle is called *your reactive cycle*. Your reactive cycle is like the trigger signature for the couple. It's good to know what it is so you can spot it when it begins.

This is what the trigger signature exercise above can uncover. When Francesca and Amy did this exercise, Francesca noted that she got triggered when Amy offered "a lot of attention" to people other than herself. She then reacted by making critical remarks about Amy's relational capacity or her capacity for commitment. In filling out her worksheet, Amy listed that her reactive behavior was to try to reason with Francesca — to tell her she was misreading the situation and explain to Francesca that these other people were just friends.

After doing the trigger signature worksheet several times about several different triggering events, they began to recognize their reactive cycle. Whenever Francesca complained or criticized, Amy would start explaining or minimizing. And the more Amy explained, the more Francesca expanded her criticisms. Then, the more Francesca did this, the more solidly and firmly Amy tried to build her case that Francesca was misreading the situation. How long can a couple go on like this before they realize they are saying the same thing in different words over and over? Partners can stay stuck in this sort of circular communication for years. But when you learn to spot your reactive cycle, while also knowing how to spot your trigger signature, then you have more resources to work with.

These exercises strengthen your noticing muscles, your capacity for mindfulness. As noticing increases, automaticity decreases. You're better equipped to call for a pause sooner rather than later. After doing the trigger signature worksheet together a few times, partners will probably see how their reactive behaviors interact to create this sort of predictable cotriggering cycle. As they strengthen their ability to notice familiar patterns, it won't take them as long to call for a pause and halt reactivity.

Another good reason for partners to recognize and label their reactive cycle is that it reinforces the idea that they are *coresponsible*. It demonstrates that you're in this together, that no one is to blame, and that either partner could interrupt the cycle at any time. You come to see that it is your mutual reactive cycle that is the problem — not your partner. The two of you have a mutually created problem that arises from your mutual inability to manage your triggers. Understanding the phenomenon of cotriggering helps you be more forgiving toward yourself and your partner. Reactive cycles happen because we are "wired together."

The only way for couples to get out of the cycle is by developing their mutual ability to pause. It's not easy for one person to halt the cycle by themselves. But when both partners take responsibility for pausing, then they have a chance.

Creating a Pause Agreement

Couples need to create a formal pause agreement. After accepting that triggers happen, learning to pause is the second most important skill in this trigger-work program.

Most couples can agree that pausing is a good idea. But after that, a lot can go wrong. The most common resistance to pausing occurs because partners simply do not recognize that they are triggered until reactivity has been going on for a while. By that time, the runaway freight train of reactivity has too much momentum. The other common resistance to pausing is not wanting to stop the conversation. Couples may believe that, even though they know they are getting triggered, they can still temper their reactions enough to resolve the issue. Generally, this is a mistake. With enough practice, your ability and willingness to pause will improve. It all starts with a clear and realistic agreement. Don't expect instant success, and don't abandon the practice after a few failures. There is a learning curve involved.

What does a pause agreement consist of? It is relatively simple and involves four steps:

1. Together, you pick a word or short phrase that will be your pause signal, such as "pause," "whoa," "time-out," or "uh-oh."

2. You both agree that if either person says this phrase, you will both immediately stop talking or doing what you're doing — no exceptions. Then you will both sit quietly and take about ten slow, conscious breaths through the nose, after which you will decide whether your pause time should be short (ten to fifteen minutes), medium (one to three hours), or long (three to eight hours).

3. During the pause, each person takes time to go inward. This involves some sort of self-calming practice (chapter 4), followed by the Compassionate Self-Inquiry practice (chapter 5), and then writing a

repair statement (chapter 6). Partners may spend the time alone, or they may stay together silently in the same room, but most people find it best to be alone.

4. Finally, after the agreed-upon time, the person who said "pause" will find the other person, and together they will decide if they are both feeling calm and resourceful enough to do their repair. If they are not, they estimate how long they will need before they are ready to repair, and they agree to check back in after that.

In some instances, people pause pretty quickly — before much reactivity takes over their nervous systems — and they find that it doesn't take much time to restore a sense of mutual safety. Just sitting next to or near each other and doing five minutes of conscious breathing may be enough. The couple may not even need to fill out a repair statement. After they get calm, one person might simply say, "I was starting to get triggered. I'm feeling safe again now. How about you?" Then, after asking for and giving a hug or some verbal reassurance, the couple can move on.

If you believe this might be the case for you, agree to a quick pause, and afterward, check to see if both of you are feeling safe and connected. If you are, then that's probably enough of a repair. Your pause did what it was supposed to do. It gave you both a chance to admit you were getting triggered, to quickly calm yourselves, and to reach out for connection.

If one partner is not too triggered, another helpful action — which can reduce nervous system activation and shorten the time needed for successful self-regulation — is for that person to say something like "I know we'll get through this." Sometimes, a few simple reassuring words like this can have a calming effect. You might also do this for yourself at the beginning of your pause time, saying to yourself, "We'll get through this." A triggered nervous system is often unable to see the bigger picture of how many times the partners have lost connection, repaired, and felt closer afterward. This simple sentence helps couples remember that they have been through a lot, and they are still together.

For any type of pause to be successful, both partners need to have some competence with the entire trigger-work curriculum, all five steps described in part 1. This includes the following: You both accept that triggering happens; you can identify your own and your partner's trigger signature and your reactive cycle; you can notice your reactive stories, core attachment fears, and core needs; you have mastered one or two self-calming practices; you have learned to practice Compassionate Self-Inquiry; you know how to fill out and deliver a repair statement; and you know how to offer the kind of reassurance that addresses your partner's core fear and core need. Becoming familiar with this whole sequence reinforces your faith in the pause practice — because you know there are constructive things you can do after the pause to restore connection and safety.

Further, both partners understand that the pause is never used to avoid discussing something. You agree that you will always check in with each other at the agreed-upon time to see if you are both ready to do your repair. And after a successful repair, then you can decide on a time when you will get back to the discussion that was underway when the triggering happened. Don't ever try to do problem-solving about the issue at hand (whether that's money, sex, or the kids) while triggered or while you are still in the repair step. Partners both need to feel calm, safe, and openhearted before they can collaborate and resolve issues. For that, you need to have your higher brain functioning online. Remember, triggering hijacks your higher brain capacities for cooperation and empathic listening. No brain, no gain.

During Your Individual Pause Time

At the start of a pause, even though you may have already done ten deep breaths with your partner, you will probably need to continue with a breathing or a body-awareness practice to fully calm your activated nervous system. You may notice your mind fixating on what happened, what was done to you, what should or shouldn't have been said or done, or on justifying why you are upset, angry, or disappointed. The goal during a pause is to discover and utilize the best practices that help you let go of, or step back from, such ruminating. With a little practice, you can learn to intentionally focus your attention on the sensations of your breathing or the sensations of being held by the chair you are sitting in. It might take a while for your mind to let go of the need to be right, validated, or agreed with. But even if the mind is active, you can still experience the calming effect of conscious breathing. Try counting your breaths, saying silently to yourself something like "Inhale, two, three, four, rest. Exhale, two, three, four, five, six, rest." Thoughts may persist in the background, but you will find your body becoming more settled and relaxed.

It can be useful to observe the mind's chatter as you continue your breathing practice during a pause. Notice, for example, how the mind will think things like: *This is a waste of time. This is not getting us any closer to resolving our issue.*

Why couldn't he just remember to call the plumber? I can't do this anymore. Watching your thoughts like this is very beneficial. The more you practice *noticing* your thoughts, instead of *identifying with* your thoughts, the easier it will be to hold a compassionate space for yourself during a pause.

As you practice watching your thoughts, you'll probably notice various thinking habits, like judging, comparing, blaming, trying to be right, or divining your partner's motives. These habits disconnect you from the deeper feelings and needs inside of you. These deeper, more vulnerable, feelings, fears, and needs must be attended to if healing is to occur.

Watching your breathing and noticing body sensations keeps your attention focused on the simple reality of this present moment — you sitting in this room in this chair. This will create a sense of inner spaciousness. The more spacious you are, the less reactive you will be.

Activating Self-Compassion During a Pause

Once you have paused long enough to bring about feelings of calmness and safety, then you are ready to spend some time relating intimately with yourself by doing the Compassionate Self-Inquiry practice (see pages 97–103). Repeatedly doing this practice — after you get triggered, during your pause — fosters an attitude of empathy, tenderness, and compassion toward the parts of yourself that feel hurt, angry, insecure, fearful, or overwhelmed. You may also come to realize that holding space for yourself like this leaves you feeling softer and more forgiving afterward — so you're in a more generous frame of mind when you meet with your partner to do your repair.

After every trigger, after every pause, take yourself through the Compassionate Self-Inquiry practice. The first twenty or so times you do it, follow all the steps described in chapter 5. After that, you will probably find yourself moving through the steps more quickly and even skipping some steps. Eventually, everything may go much more quickly, including the pause, self-calming, and creating a compassionate "holding space" for your tender self. With practice, as I note above, sometimes all you need is to tell your partner, "I'm triggered. I need a moment," and all the steps that used to take twenty to thirty minutes or more can take place in less than a minute of internal "being with."

Asking for Help During Repair

Your repair will go well if you have done all the steps leading up to it and have filled out your repair statement before meeting with your partner. If your repair does not go well, it may be because you have not yet mastered one or more of the earlier steps. Usually, the acceptance step is hardest to master. If you have resistance to accepting that getting triggered arises from your own wounding, trauma, or unfinished business, you will still be holding a blaming story or a story that your partner should have or could have behaved differently. Your focus will be on what the other person failed to do, and the conversation will have a fault-finding dynamic. When this happens, pause to give yourself some tenderness. Recognize that it's really hard to feel your own upset and to accept that triggering happened, and it left you feeling hurt, angry, or insecure. The human ego-mind seems addicted to finding reasons and passing judgment, so it's not easy to just feel what we feel, without our thoughts coming in to complicate things.

The repair statement gives you practice owning that a core fear got triggered and asking for your partner's help to address that fear. It's really important to accept and own up to the fact that, when you are triggered, you are not able to see the whole picture. You may be seeing things through the lens of your insecurities, and sometimes you need your partner's help.

If you tend to deny your need for reassurance or help, then during Compassionate Self-Inquiry, try spending some time focusing on that part of yourself. Recognize any fears about feeling incompetent, not enough, needy, inept, weak, not perfect, flawed, powerless, helpless, or dependent on someone else. Start by imagining this part of you as needing help but being unable to ask for it or unable to believe that help is available. Notice the feelings and sensations that arise. Pay attention to any changes you notice. Breathe deeply. Feel your own spacious presence, holding space for memories and associations to arise. Be curious. Ask questions of this part, and see what this part feels and what it needs. You might try writing an inner dialogue in your journal between the part of you that has disdain for weakness and the part of you that needs help. This is another way to strengthen self-compassion. It helps you have a better, more supportive relationship with yourself. The better your relationship is with yourself, the better your relationships with others will be, and the less dependent you will be on others.

The essence of repair is owning that you reacted automatically; admitting the fear that prompted this reaction; reassuring your partner that what you did, thought, or said while triggered was *not* your deepest truth; asking for help or reassurance; and receiving reassurance. Repeatedly asking for, and getting, reassurance will eventually heal any fear of emotional pain and rewire any insecure brain circuitry — because you are allowing yourself to receive the type of loving attention that you did not get enough of during a critical time in your development. To receive help, you need to admit that you need help.

Subliminal or Nonobvious Triggers

Long-term intimate relationships can develop unhealthy patterns that may go unnoticed for many years. In addition to recognizing reactive cycles, look out for these less obvious bad habits.

Intimate partners become subconsciously attuned to what pleases and displeases their partner. Each person feels safe when their partner is happy, in a good mood, or attending to them. They feel less safe when their partner is upset or not attending to them. At the extreme, this can develop into a codependent relationship, in which each person focuses so much on their partner's state that they lose touch with their own authentic feelings and needs. Each person tries to please and appease their partner rather than be true to themselves. Partnerships vary quite a bit with regard to how codependent they are.

This relates to the survival alarm system in our brains, which is always scanning for rifts in connection with "the one we depend on." Over time, if rifts go unrepaired and reactive fear-stories go unexamined, partners can come to see each other through the lens of their core fear. They think things like "I don't matter to them," "I'm too much," "I'm a disappointment," "I'm not enough." After a while, people can come to believe that their fear-story is true, and they become very sensitive to anything their partner does that even remotely relates to this unconscious fear/belief. They "see" evidence of it everywhere. They no longer feel safe, as if there are land mines everywhere. Both partners may live in a chronic state of vigilance, anxiety, or lack of ease. But they aren't conscious of this because they've gotten so used to it. The truth is they are both subliminally triggered pretty much all of the time. To fix this problem, they need to bring more awareness to subtle signs of triggering in their partnership.

Subtle Signs of Triggering

There are many subtle signs of triggering that most people would not recognize as trigger reactions. These subtle irritants can increase over time if unrepaired ruptures mount. For example, say a woman asks her partner to sit down and talk. He agrees, but he does not show the level of enthusiasm that the woman is hoping for. So she thinks, *He really doesn't want to talk*, and she tells him, "Hey, it can wait." Due to her lifelong insecurities, plus a backlog of unrepaired relationship ruptures between them, she has gotten to the point where she is vigilant for any sign that she is not important to him. She sees "rejection" everywhere. She does not entertain the possibility that his modest level of enthusiasm may have nothing to do with how he feels about her request.

While the woman in this example doesn't have an obvious reaction, she is triggered nonetheless. When she says, "It can wait," that is a reactive behavior based on a reactive story. In this case, the fear-story is that her partner really does not want to talk, that he's not really interested in her, that she doesn't matter or is not very important to him. She doesn't reveal these fears because she may not even be aware of them herself. She reacts automatically, having gotten into the habit of watching his reactions carefully for signs of disinterest. Her fear-story guides her expectations and actions, and pretty soon she may stop asking for attention altogether, or she may only ask in very indirect ways. With every incident like this one, the woman's fear-story gets reinforced, becoming more and more entrenched in her unconscious mind. She preemptively chooses not to expect too much, not to depend on him, and not to trust that he cares. Eventually, she will develop an unconscious pattern of leaving him alone and not asking for much.

As distancing habits like this continue, partners feel less safe and more guarded with each other. Many couples suffer through this type of communication every day, thinking this is just the way it is. Over time, unexamined reactive stories may get expanded; in this example, the woman might come to view her partner as self-centered, uncaring, even narcissistic.

If you suspect that you and your partner have become accustomed to living with subliminal triggers, it's time to have a serious talk. Here are some ideas for how to approach this talk:

1. Start by saying you want to explore whether subliminal triggering is occurring between you. If your partner doesn't know what this is, explain the concept: Over time in a relationship, partners collect data about which bids for attention or connection work well and which not so well. Partners use this data to assess what's safe to bring up, and they may stop asking for the things they think the partner cannot give or is not interested in giving. Ask your partner what they think of this idea, and share your own thoughts, plus any specific examples you notice from your relationship.

2. Emphasize that one result of this dynamic is that people often express their needs indirectly. The wife doesn't come right out and say to her husband, "You are working long hours, and this leaves me alone with the kids a lot. I miss you. I need to feel we're a team. I want you to work less and spend more time with us." She might merely hint, criticize, or complain without directly *asking* in an openhearted way. Invite your partner to consider whether you both might be guilty of indirect asking.

3. Then invite your partner to have a conversation focused on a series of questions that you both ask of yourselves. Start by asking, "What was I hoping for or wanting when we first got together that I have stopped wanting or expecting?" Before you begin sharing your responses, be sure your nervous system is calm and relaxed and your mind is open and curious. Be ready to pause and self-calm at the first sign of triggering. Take turns being the talker and the listener. Do not interrupt, and perhaps agree that each person gets five minutes, more or less. After you have both had a turn to talk, debrief this step of the exercise. Each person should share what they noticed about their feelings, sensations, and self-talk during the exercise — for example, did any familiar fears come up? You may want to take a break before going on to the next question.

4. Next, consider the question: "Can you recall at least one specific situation where you wanted something from your partner (such as time with them or time away from them), but you were pretty sure

you knew what your partner's response would be, so you did not mention it?" Again, both of you should answer and take turns talking and listening.

5. Finally, consider the specific incidents you each just named and ask yourselves: "If I could do it over, and if I felt completely safe that I could deal with your answer, no matter what it was, how might I ask for what I want or express my need or concern? What would I actually say?"

6. After you have both responded to and discussed your answers to these questions, share ideas about how to help each other feel safer to ask for time or attention (or anything). If triggering happens during this, be ready to pause, self-calm, self-soothe, and repair. Then, debrief the whole exercise — giving each other time to share what you noticed about your own feelings, sensations, stories, and triggers.

Partners who regularly check in with each other like this find that it gets easier over time to speak about and listen to difficult disclosures. Fears get reassured. The need to defend, protect, or play it safe dissolves. And paradoxically, the less you play it safe, the safer you both feel.

Chapter Eight

I'm Triggered with My Kids

*Being a parent has certain built-in dynamics that
can be a setup for recurring trigger reactions.*

Anyone who has ever been a parent has had moments
of feeling impatient, frustrated, disappointed, or overwhelmed in relationship to their child. And every child has
probably felt some of these things toward their parents. But as
the parent, you're the one your child depends on. You're the
one who is expected to be the adult, the one who is supposed
to know how to manage difficult situations competently. So
how can you square this with the fact that sometimes you
don't feel very adultlike? Sometimes you don't know what to
do. Sometimes you may even feel like giving up. This chapter
discusses how to handle triggering with children — focusing
primarily on younger kids who still live at home and are financial dependents. That said, much of this can also be applied to

situations involving adult children who live outside the family home.

Parenting as a Practice

Earlier, I suggested approaching intimate relationships as a practice — a path to inner development and healing, a psychospiritual journey. This goes for the parent-child relationship as much as it does for couples. But there is one big difference. In parenting, your child is not your equal. It is not a give-and-take relationship in the usual sense. It's more like you give and the child takes. That's one reason being a parent can be triggering.

Being a parent has certain built-in dynamics that can be a setup for recurring trigger reactions. In working with parents and families, I have identified three of the most common causes of parental triggering:

1. It's not fair. What about my needs?
2. My kid's deficits trigger me.
3. I don't understand my kid.

What About My Needs?

Most people have kids before they figure out how to be a good parent to their own inner child. They still have a lot of unmet needs themselves and can become easily frustrated when things don't go their way. So when they have a child, whose needs for attention can be quite taxing, there are plenty of opportunities for triggering. It's as if some hidden part of the parent is saying, *What about me? What about my needs?*

I think this issue is way more common than parents like

to admit: They're not doing that great at meeting their own needs, and they have this little person who is constantly demanding attention. At first, it's the parents' need for sleep versus the baby's need to be fed or held. Then, it's the need to get things done versus the toddler's need to be bathed, changed, clothed, entertained, and kept safe. Most parents expect it to be this way, but then it never seems to end, and it can become harder to accept making such sacrifices.

If you or your spouse complain a lot, this is a sign that your own needs are not being met and that you are frequently in a triggered state. Complaining signals that we want something we're not getting. Maybe we want more help or appreciation from our spouse. Maybe we just want a break or a nap. Maybe we wish our child was more self-reliant or not as needy. Or maybe so much of our partner's attention is going into parenting that we feel neglected or left out.

A Healing Exercise for Parents

If any of these examples feel familiar to you, take a moment to reflect on how well your own needs are being met: your need for help, teamwork, cooperation; your need to feel appreciated or valued; your need to feel that you are doing enough or are good enough. Do any of these needs strike a resonant chord within you? If so, try this self-nurturing exercise:

Start by focusing on a specific need or a specific memory of a time when, in your role as a parent, this need was not being met (such as the need to feel valued or appreciated). Recall a general sense of how this need feels, or bring back the specific memory, and notice your body sensations and feelings.

As in the Compassionate Self-Inquiry practice (see pages

97–103), be sure you are breathing fully and deeply in order to support whatever feelings arise. As your breathing opens up and becomes more spacious, take the attitude or stance of a big, open, nurturing presence holding space for the feelings associated with this unmet need.

Notice the body sensations of your breathing as you also welcome any other sensations that arise — sensations that seem to be associated with the unmet need you are experiencing. Allow memories or past associations to come up. You might recall a childhood memory where one of your developmental needs for protection, safety, loving attention, or support was not met. If this occurs, recall how you as that child felt back then; let the witnessing part of you tenderly embrace the child part. See if you can activate your own inner good mother who can hold a nurturing, accepting space for whatever your inner child feels.

Be with yourself like this for a while, as you offer comfort, tenderness, and empathy to the part of you that feels unmet or unsupported or to the unmet need. See if you can feel compassion or *sorrow* for yourself — for your inner child or for how busy or stressed out you feel. This is different from feeling *sorry for yourself.* This type of sorrow is a form of self-empathy.

If blaming, shaming, or guilty thoughts arise, continue to witness these thoughts from the position of a compassionate observer. Come back to noticing feelings and body sensations. If tears come, allow these. Reassure yourself that your feelings are understandable, that it's okay to feel this way.

Allow these feelings to be witnessed and held for a while, as you continue to breathe fully and deeply. After a while, you will get a sense of relaxation and relief or a sense that you are not alone, that you can be there for yourself. Your external circumstances may remain unchanged, but your relationship to your circumstances will feel different. It's as if you have gotten a new perspective on your situation. You have taken one more step toward coming to terms with your present situation. Doing this self-compassion exercise repeatedly offers another step toward healing your fear or shame about being emotionally upset, in distress, or in pain.

Self-compassion is the key to becoming a more genuinely loving parent. As you practice being generous and empathetic with yourself, your expectations of yourself, of your kid, of others, and of life itself become more realistic — which means you no longer suffer when things are not the way you think they should be or could be. This is how you quell the inner voices that tell you something's wrong, either with you or with your kid. This is how the path of parenting becomes one version of the hero's journey, the journey of awakening.

I'm Triggered by My Kid's Deficits

As parents watch their children grow up, they notice the ways their kids excel and the ways they don't, what they prefer and what they avoid, their good habits and their less helpful traits. A child might be sedentary, preferring screen time to playing outdoors. They might easily put on weight. They may be highly sensitive and have their feelings easily hurt. They may have trouble cooperating with others and always need to get their way. Maybe a child has tantrums, or develops tics or stutters, or wets the bed, and parents fear these things signal underlying psychological issues. A child might be painfully shy, or afraid to take risks, or have trouble developing close friendships, and it's not clear why.

Parents may find that certain behaviors in their kid remind them of things they don't like about themselves, their spouse, or other family members. Parents might be reminded of their own parents and of dysfunctional behaviors they experienced growing up. Many adults, for example, had parents who did not have good self-care habits or who were immature or addicted. When parents see these things showing up in their children, this can be triggering.

It can be especially difficult for a parent to watch a child growing up with the same self-defeating habits or weaknesses that they had as a youngster or that they still have. Here is a good illustration from a family I used to know:

One day, Steve watched the neighborhood kids getting ready for a pickup softball game. His ten-year-old son, Tommy, was among the group that was waiting to be picked for a team. As sides were being chosen by the two captains, it was obvious to Steve that neither side was eager to have frail, unathletic Tommy on their team. As Tommy tried to hold back his tears, Steve gave his son an encouraging look. But deep inside, Steve's own shame was triggered, since he had a core fear of not being good enough. As a kid, Steve felt weak, unathletic, and lacking in confidence, and this feeling had continued into adulthood. Now, as a parent, he was doing his best to make sure Tommy did not follow in those footsteps. Steve did not want Tommy to suffer through adolescence as he had suffered. As Steve watched the game unfold, he did not want to feel shame about his son, but he couldn't help it. Whenever he saw Tommy give up on things without trying (as Steve himself still sometimes did), Steve would get triggered. Whenever he saw Tommy making careless mistakes that showed he was not really paying attention, Steve would get triggered — even though, once again, he knew this was one of his own weaknesses.

If you get triggered by something in your kid that reminds you of one of your own deficits, this can be the starting point for some useful self-inquiry and healing. It might even provide an opening toward deeper communication with your child, depending on your child's intellectual and emotional maturity.

If your child has a fairly good emotional vocabulary and is over the age of ten, I recommend that you have an open discussion with the child about your triggers and insecurities or about your own strengths and weaknesses. This could lead into a broader discussion about how everyone has things they are good at and not so good at, and how hard it can be to admit weaknesses. But don't initiate this discussion until you have worked with the tools in this book for a while and can accept your own deficits. The goal is to learn to become less perfectionistic — to accept that we all have "growth edges," weaknesses, and things we're not good at.

Exercise: Identifying Your Deficits

Whether you are a parent or not, take some time to make a list of your personal strengths and weaknesses. This doesn't need to be comprehensive; just name a few strengths and a few weaknesses. Then, if you are a parent, make a similar list of your child's strengths and weaknesses. Then compare the lists — your own and your child's — and note the similarities and differences among the strengths and weaknesses. Make a note where you and your child share the same weakness or where you have a strength and your child has a deficit. These are red flags. Either of these two circumstances can set the stage for you, the parent, to become triggered. If your spouse (or the other parent) is available, try including them in the exercise.

Then choose one of the attributes you flagged and do the following exercise. As with all trigger-work exercises, begin by sitting comfortably and allowing your breathing to deepen. Self-calm and close your eyes if this feels right.

1. Recall a specific situation when your child's behavior seemed to be an expression of this deficit, or when you were triggered seeing this behavior. Bring the whole scene to mind.

2. Allow yourself to reexperience the feelings and body sensations, recalling both your inner and outer reactions. Notice what thoughts, self-talk, assumptions, judgments, worries, or fear-stories arise.

3. Stay with these feelings, thoughts, and sensations for a while as you expand your inner sense of spaciousness, making space for any uncomfortable feelings, sensations, or thoughts to just be there. Notice if a particular feeling or thought comes to the foreground. Notice if anything moves, changes, gets more intense, less intense, or dissolves.

4. If feelings ever get too intense, back off from being with the feelings, and look around the room you are in. Name and describe one or two objects in the room.

5. Notice how you, the observer, are relating to the things that are arising in your awareness. Are you feeling relaxed and open? Or are you more resistant toward your inner experience? You can tell you are resistant when there is bodily tension or contraction, or when thoughts are critical or judgmental.

6. If resistance comes up, see if you can embrace this resistance as a part of you that needs to be acknowledged. Allow yourself to become curious about this resistance. Is there a body sensation or a body posture associated with the resistance? Allow all of this to simply be present as part of your experience.

7. If resistance does not come up, or if the resistance dissolves, continue to welcome whatever arises. See if any memories or associations come up. If memories from your own past, including your childhood, arise, hold this younger version of you with empathy or tenderness.

8. See if you can imagine that this tender part of you needs something. What does it need? In your imagination, think of yourself as a big nurturing presence, and ask it what it needs from you. You may or may not get a clear answer. This is not as important as the fact that you are offering supportive attention to your inner child, or to the part of you experiencing distress, discomfort, or shame.

9. Be with yourself like this for a while. Breathe fully and deeply. Feel the support of the chair you are sitting on. When you are ready to bring this to a close, open your eyes and look around, stretch, move, or get up and walk around.

Connecting the Dots

After completing this reflection, consider how the triggering thing your kid did relates to your own deficits or to a deficit in your own parents or your spouse. Do you find any similarities between one of your deficits and your kid's triggering behavior? Or is there an area of life where you are especially capable and your kid is not? When you do this exercise, does it bring you to a place of greater acceptance within yourself? The goal of the exercise is to give you practice bringing spacious awareness and compassionate witnessing to anything that distresses you. Any difficult-to-accept situation can be the starting point for inquiry. Once you learn to view parenting as a practice, you don't expect your life to go any particular way. You take distressing events and unwanted surprises as natural. These things show up and you handle them. Triggers happen. And when they happen, you use these as a doorway to deeper self-experiencing and self-knowledge.

While doing this exercise, a parent may find that their kid's triggering behavior reminds them of how one of their parents behaved toward them when they were younger. For example, say the child behaves in an unyielding way, which triggers the parent, and in the exercise, the parent connects with their own inner child who felt dominated or controlled by their own parents. This explains why the parent may often feel manipulated or controlled, and thus triggered, by their child. Once the parent sees this connection, they know that their inner work as a parent includes confronting their fear of feeling manipulated, controlled, or unheard. Maybe it appears ridiculous, to others or to the parent, that they could feel powerless in relationship to their kid, but trigger reactions are not logical. Trigger reactions represent faulty associations in our development that affect our brain wiring. In this instance, if the person, as a child, had a parent with a dominating personality, they may have learned to fear confrontation or conflict with this parent. When they stood up to this parent, the parent got upset or angry — which was quite scary. They may have imagined that standing up to their parent would lead to emotional abandonment, which made strong assertion unthinkable. As a result, they became an agreeable, adaptable little person who avoided conflict and confrontation at all cost. This sort of personality pattern — the pattern of adapting rather than asserting — can last a lifetime. An adult might realize that their own kid would not abandon them, but they might still feel a sense of fear or dread whenever there was a potential conflict. The parent's fear of feeling emotionally separate or abandoned might still get triggered. Of course, such fears can be healed, but this takes practice.

As another example, maybe the parent is triggered because they see their kid engaging in behaviors — like poor self-care habits — that are self-defeating or that may lead to trouble in adulthood. Yet this is an area of life where the parent excels. The parent is fit and active and worries that their kid is becoming fat and lazy. The parent gets triggered when they catch their kid sneaking junk food. They feel helpless, out of control, and ineffectual. This is painful. What can a parent do? The most important thing is to give one's own pain the space to be compassionately witnessed.

If this situation applies to you, see if you can accept that it is painful to watch your kid sometimes. Your heart hurts when you see them not succeeding in the ways you want for them. If this feeling weighs on you, allow yourself to have whatever feelings you have, be tender toward yourself, and over time, the weight will become a little lighter. If we want to positively influence our children, it works best to first clear away the distorted thinking that triggering causes in our own brain. Then, we are more likely to communicate with our kids in ways they can emotionally connect with and trust.

I Don't Understand My Kid

Children sometimes behave in unexpected ways — ways that seem odd or unusual to their parents. Sometimes this discrepancy shows up right away — like when a parent likes to cuddle their baby, but the baby fights this. Most often it shows up later in the child's development. In multi-child households, these differences may not be so distressing, but when parents only have one child, they are more likely to get triggered by "unusual" behavior.

There are so many different examples of how a parent and child can be "wired" differently. A parent may be very scientific and data-oriented and their kid might seem like a dreamer, operating mainly from intuition. A father may be a "man's man" and have a son who is more androgynous. A parent may be carefree and upbeat but have a kid who seems worried a lot.

If you and your kid have a difference like this, it can be a unique growth opportunity. The situation can force you to grow beyond any limited or self-oriented views of how people should be. It may help you come to terms with the fact that what motivates you is not necessarily what motivates others.

If having a kid who seems different from you causes you distress, I suggest exploring a book on personality types, such as the Myers-Briggs Type Indicator or the Enneagram system of types. These can help people understand the types of people whose behavior might not make sense to them.

Dealing with a parent-child difference in temperament can help you learn to live well in a world of different personality types. Most people naively expect others to react basically the way they themselves do. Whatever your personality type, I urge you to become curious about the vulnerabilities and blind spots of that type, while realizing that everyone can grow or evolve beyond their type. Your type is not a life sentence. It's the result of genetics and conditioning. People can learn and change as they continue along the parenting path or any other relationship path. Having a kid who seems different can feel confronting, and it can be frustrating. But it can also be a huge gift for personal growth.

How to Repair with Your Kid

Whatever the reason, if you get actively triggered by your kid, you will need to do your inner work and then initiate a repair as soon as possible. It may help to remember how it was for you as a kid when one of your parents got upset with you. Most people recall feeling afraid, unsafe, and even terrified at times. What did you need after that happened? Most kids would say that they need reassurance that they are loved; whatever happened, they want to know the parent is over it and feeling affectionate toward them.

In my own childhood, I was fairly lucky in this regard. Although my dad often popped off at me in anger, and I would get frozen in fear, he would always come to find me fairly soon afterward and tell me he was sorry he overreacted. Sometimes he would tell me that my behavior had scared him because he feared I might hurt myself (like the time I almost ran into the street in front of an oncoming car). Sometimes he would say he didn't know why he reacted the way he did, but it wasn't because of anything bad or wrong about me. These apologies meant so much to me. As I think about this now, my eyes fill with tears of gratitude. When he would get angry, I thought he didn't love me anymore. But he didn't allow me to sit for too long with this fear. He was adult enough to calm himself, empathize with my fears and needs, take responsibility for his reactive behavior, and reassure me of his love.

When it comes to your own repair with your kid, the exact words you use for your repair script will depend on the child's age or maturity. The words my dad started out with were, "I'm sorry I lost my temper." And even at five years old, I knew what he meant. Nowadays, you could probably introduce this concept to a child of five and tie it in with the idea that we all need a "time-out" now and then to calm down after we get upset. The word *upset* may be a good, generic term to use. Follow this with the idea that once we are calm, then we should apologize or repair. After you have taught your kid this much, after a little while, you can add the idea of the do-over (as in, "If I could do it over..."). Of course, the best way to teach this is to model it. But a brief explanation sets the expectation that this is how people who love one another handle things like anger and other rifts in connection. Here is the repair statement I suggest when addressing a child between the ages of five and eighteen:

I'd like to apologize for _____ [insert your reactive behavior, such as: *yelling, hitting you, calling you a name, slamming the door, ignoring you,* and so on].

I am sorry I did [or said] that. I didn't mean to.

Optional: I was triggered. [Say this only if your child already understands the concept of being triggered, but do not say this to minimize or excuse bad behavior.]

I want you to know I am over being upset and that I love you very much. [Accompany this with a gentle hug or ask, "Can we have a hug?"]

Once you have delivered this repair statement to your child, notice whether the child seems relaxed or tense. If they seem tense, ask them about it, saying: "Did I scare you?" or "Are you still upset with me?" Make sure you are feeling open and spacious before you ask this question. Give your child plenty of time to answer. If you keep talking after you ask the question, you will give the impression that you do not really want an honest answer. If your child admits to still being scared, offer empathy and understanding — the same things you would offer to your own inner child.

When children learn that upsets can be healed, this helps them grow up willing to take emotional risks in the interest of intimacy. They will be less guarded, defended, or secretive with the people they care about — because they know that we sometimes unintentionally hurt others or get hurt, but that such things are forgivable and repairable.

Chapter Nine

I'm Triggered
with My Friend

A friendship where two people view their rela-
tionship as a growth practice can offer the same
opportunity for healing childhood wounds that a
marriage can.

Many close friendships have a sibling dynamic — characterized by rivalry, comparison, or competition. Some
have the same pursuer-versus-pursued dynamic as occurs in
intimate couples. But even in less complicated friendships,
when there is a difference in needs, values, expectations, or
personality styles, triggering often happens.

Sharon and Taylor were meeting at a café for lunch. As
soon as they sat down, Taylor started complaining about some
difficulties she was having with another friend, whom Sharon
didn't know. Sharon pretended to be interested, but she was
really feeling disappointed that Taylor seemed more interested
in this other friend than in her. Even as their conversation

moved on to other topics, Sharon was not very present. After they said goodbye, Sharon realized she had been triggered the whole time. She had gone into a mini-freeze reaction, where words continued to come out of her mouth, and her face continued to smile at appropriate times, but she was clearly not all there.

When she got home and paused to feel her feelings more fully, she realized that her fear of being invisible or unimportant had been triggered. When she took time to do the Compassionate Self-Inquiry practice, she connected with a familiar feeling from childhood. She remembered several occasions when she had expressed a desire or an opinion, hoping to get a caring response from her older brother or her mother. But instead, they often responded with something completely unrelated to what Sharon had said, leaving her with a sense of being invisible. This happened to her often enough that she developed a core fear of being insignificant, invisible, unimportant. She learned to deal with this unconscious fear by shutting down and shutting up, thus becoming even more invisible — to herself as well as to others.

Choosing How to Respond to a Friend

If you were Sharon, what might you do or say about this incident with your friend? Would you confront Taylor about how insensitive she can be sometimes? Would you vow to be more aware of your trigger signature in the future, so you can catch your reactions sooner? Would you use this incident as an opportunity to bring compassion to this tender part of you, with the aim of gradually increasing your self-acceptance and gradually decreasing your resistance to feeling difficult feelings? Would you go back to Taylor to clear the air or repair, revealing to her that this fear got triggered, that you shut down, and that you'd like reassurance that you are important to her? Would you decide that Taylor triggers you too much, and it's best to just avoid her from now on? These are all possible options.

The choice you make will depend on whether your primary aim is to avoid discomfort or to heal and grow when things like this occur. Whenever you have a difficult choice to make regarding what to say or do in an interpersonal relationship, first ask yourself this question: What is my aim? Is it to use the relationship as a crucible for both of us to heal, learn, become inwardly stronger, and know ourselves and each other more deeply? Or is it to keep the peace, appear strong, avoid upsets, stay comfortable, feel in control, or be validated? In my book *Getting Real* (about how to express your authentic self), I raise this same important question, which I frame slightly differently: "Is the intent of your communication to *relate* (to know and be known, which can be risky and leads to growth) or to *control* (to manage and minimize discomfort, which is the default position for most people)?"

In any situation where you are triggered by a friend, you might also consider two other questions: Can my nervous system handle it if this trigger keeps coming up in this relationship? And does my friend value *relating* as a path? To answer the first question, reflect on your past experience: Is it retraumatizing to you when things like "feeling unimportant" occur? Do you take a long time to recover? To answer the second question, assuming your friend is someone you'd like to relate to more deeply, I suggest asking: Do they value using relationship upsets as opportunities to work with and repair trigger reactions, and do they have the inner resilience to do this? In other words, can they bounce back after an upsetting conversation? Can they handle hearing that you are displeased with something they've done?

A friendship where two people view their relationship as a growth practice can offer the same opportunity for healing childhood wounds that a marriage can. The trigger-work tools can be helpful in any type of relationship. In most friendships, the two people are not as interdependent as marriage partners (they don't live together or have kids together), so generally, they should expect to have fewer conflicts. But sometimes, a friend will come along who really pushes our buttons. Since there is less at stake, it may be less stressful to work with one's triggers in this type of relationship.

On the other hand, having less at stake also means people are not as motivated to stick it out. It is easier to back away from a friendship than to end a marriage. If you try using these tools with a friend, and you find this relationship is too hard on your nervous system, it is really okay to back away or redefine the terms of the relationship. It's okay to avoid getting retraumatized or to admit there is a limit to the amount of emotional intensity you want to deal with. People vary quite a bit in how much interpersonal intensity they prefer and how much they can tolerate. If you consider yourself a lightweight, don't get in the ring with a heavyweight. I, myself, am a bit of a lightweight in comparison to some of my friends. I think it's better to admit this than to live in constant stress. It's okay to break off friendships or to limit them to certain lengths of time or certain activities. But don't blame the other person if this is your choice. This is part of the inner work of acceptance, which is to grow beyond the blaming mindset.

Sometimes, you may not wish to engage in the level of asser-
tiveness that a particular relationship requires.

If you want to invite a friend to treat your friendship as a
process for learning, growth, and deeper relating, here's how
you might get the conversation started. Say something like
"I've been on a path to uncover and learn to work with my
emotional triggers. My friendships are one place my triggers
show up. You're a good friend, so I want to ask if you'd like
to create some mutual agreements to notice and reveal when
we get triggered, and maybe to even repair or clear the air
afterward. This way, we both learn about ourselves and grow
together, and we don't build up hurts or resentments. Is this
something you might want, and do you have any questions?"

If the friend agrees, perhaps suggest they read this book,
particularly part 1, so that they understand the repair process
as well as you do. If you and your friend decide to move in
this direction, expect a lot of trial and error at first, so use
this book to guide you on this path. In addition, you and
your friend might also want to read one of my other books
that discuss triggers and relationships: see *Getting Real* (2001),
Saying What's Real (2005), and *Five-Minute Relationship Repair*
(2015).

Avoiding Retraumatization

When deciding how to handle friendships that are triggering,
be honest and compassionate with yourself, and make choices
that avoid retraumatization. In this book, I suggest approaching daily life as a practice, which includes friendships. By
"practice," I mean approaching what shows up in your life
with an attitude of mindful compassion so that you learn to

accept and be with unpleasant feelings. The aim is to become inwardly stronger and calmer so you can face life's challenges with more courage and equanimity. But don't push yourself too hard as you are learning to do this. Don't hurt yourself by staying too long in states of discomfort. There's a time for retreating as well as advancing. Sometimes we need to withdraw into the safety or quiet of our own home, our own room, or our own inner sanctuary.

When a friendship becomes consistently stressful or triggering, I recommend disengaging for a while to get centered. This is especially important if you have suffered multiple traumas in your life or suffer from complex PTSD that is close to the surface. In some situations, it is retraumatizing to have to repeatedly mark boundaries or deal with broken agreements. You may need to disengage or mark boundaries without much (or any) explanation. Sometimes the act of explaining can be too stressful for your nervous system. The inner work required to maintain a particular friendship may be too much. So even though you may have a strong bias toward "working things out" with the important people in your life, sometimes this is not the wisest course.

For example, Irene suffered early sexual abuse and other developmental trauma, and she decided to break off a long-term friendship with Louise because interactions with Louise were becoming too stressful. Louise had a habit of angrily complaining to Irene about her sex life with her husband. Over the history of their friendship, Irene had repeatedly asked Louise to refrain from complaining about this particular subject matter, but the triggering behavior continued. It seemed that Louise was using the friendship to process her own triggers with her husband, but this was retraumatizing to Irene. It was difficult for Louise to understand Irene's sensitivity because she herself was more thick-skinned and casual about sex. Irene began noticing how every time she and Louise got together, her nervous system experienced a sense of panic or impending doom. She found herself too frozen to adequately explain this to Louise. So one day, after another interaction where Irene got frustrated trying to assert this boundary, she simply told Louise she could not be her friend anymore. To protect her own tender nervous system, Irene did this without much explanation. She thought any conversation, even a short one, would overload her. This is an unfortunate situation, but sometimes cutting off a friendship is all we can do.

Even if our own deficits are partly responsible for our inability to feel safe, and even if the other person didn't do anything wrong, sometimes our physical health and stress level should take precedence over other considerations. If you decide to end a friendship, just try to be as kind and nonblaming as you can, with both yourself and the other person. Whenever I have decided to limit or end a friendship, I have always viewed it as a limitation in my own ability to "love what is" or to assert my boundaries.

When a Friend Decides to End It with You

Now let's consider this type of situation from the other perspective. A friend gets upset or triggered in a conversation with you and decides to end the friendship, and they don't say why. This friend might not tell you even if you ask. Maybe the friend doesn't know why, or it could be because they don't feel safe to reveal some earlier trauma, like childhood sexual or physical abuse. It's very common for survivors not to disclose this. They generally go along to get along. When triggered, they freeze. But then sometimes, they get aggressive. Their behavior might be confusing, so you're often not sure where they stand or what they really need.

This can be triggering. But then, if you have an overt trigger reaction, or attempt a repair, this might upset or retraumatize your friend. Like Louise, you might find yourself on the receiving end of an abrupt breakup — without any clear understanding of why. This is a tough situation, but it can happen. Since most friendships do not have a "till death do us part" clause, people do not feel as committed to working things out as they do in a marriage. If you wish to prevent abrupt breakups from happening with a friend, one option is to create an up-front agreement about this. You agree not to end things without at least several hours of deep listening to each other's point of view.

If you ever find yourself in Louise's position, do the Compassionate Self-Inquiry practice, and repeat this every time you feel the hurt or confusion of the unexplained breakup. Make space for your inner witness to feel empathy for your hurting self. Try not to blame yourself. Remember, our emotional pain is like the tender part of us that was not allowed to cry itself out. It was not given tenderness and compassion — so it got split off from the rest of our personality and took up residence in the shadows of our subconscious mind. Trigger reactions offer us a way to reconnect with our lost or rejected parts. When these pained or hurting parts are embraced, they do not need to keep calling attention to themselves. It's like picking up and feeding a hungry, screaming baby. Usually, they stop screaming.

Repairing with Friends

When triggered by friends, most people first practice a unilateral pause (see "If the Other Person Is Triggered and Cannot Pause," pages 80–82). So the pause would be a silent, undisclosed event; you would find a way to leave the room or remove yourself, such as by going to the bathroom. Or you might initiate a unilateral pause by saying, "I'm getting overwhelmed and need to collect myself," or even, "I'm starting to get triggered. I need to pause."

Then, after you feel calm and safe again, you could come back and perhaps offer a brief repair statement, such as, "I'm sorry I had to interrupt us. I'm ready to listen now." Or if you are not yet ready to reengage, find time to do the self-compassion practice, and see how you feel after that.

Ideally, particularly with someone you trust, I suggest doing all five trigger-work steps, including pausing, self-calming, self-soothing, and repair. This requires some explanation and discussion, so that both people know what the practice entails. The repair statement may need to be modified or simplified so that the level of disclosure is appropriate for this relationship. For instance, you might not include your core fear nor make a request for reassurance beyond asking for a simple acknowledgment of understanding.

In some friendships, you might only agree to pause and self-calm when triggered and leave the other trigger-work steps out. Later, you can do self-inquiry on your own, when you are alone. Once you have some practice with these tools, it is easy to customize the pause-calm-inquire-repair process to fit each unique situation.

Finally, for certain friendships that are particularly close and important, friends may want to commit to the same process I recommend for couples in chapter 7. This can work well for people who do not have a significant other, or for friendships that are as long-lasting and intimate as a marriage. In this case, during the repair step, you would reveal the core fear that got triggered, reveal how this relates to childhood trauma, and ask for help or reassurance to assuage this fear. If you do find a friend who is willing to do this shared practice with you, you are very fortunate. I think those of us who do these practices are making a real contribution to healing the fears that divide our world.

Chapter Ten

I'm Triggered
in a Group or Meeting

Adult groups often mirror some of the dynamics of our early family, school, or peer-group experiences.

This chapter provides guidance for how to deal with your own and other people's trigger reactions in group settings. Groups provide a powerful context for working through social anxiety, authority issues, conformity issues, and issues of belonging — even if this is not the stated purpose of the group.

Getting triggered in a group can be an unforgettable experience — unforgettably uncomfortable — because there may be a lot of people you don't know very well or people you don't trust who have just witnessed you losing it! This can offer the opportunity to work with things like shame, embarrassment, conformity pressure, scapegoating, feeling left out, feeling judged, performance anxiety, and feeling not good enough.

Triggering that occurs in a group setting can be especially

powerful (and hard to manage) if our early wounding occurred in a dysfunctional family setting or an unfortunate grade school or high school experience. Adult groups often mirror some of the dynamics of our early family, school, or peer-group experiences. This is because we get conditioned, or "trained," to behave in particular ways or to take on particular group roles in these settings. Once we're adults in a group with other adults, we may unconsciously revert to the same group role we played in our childhood family, in school, or on the playground. Our role in our early family might have been the black sheep, the golden child, daddy's girl, momma's boy, the family scapegoat, mother's helper, the rescuer, the sickly one, the rebel, or the parentified child. When humans are under stress, it is natural to revert to old habits.

Family Roles

What was your role or function in your first groups — in family, church, school, in the neighborhood, and so on? Did you seek the limelight or avoid it? Did you lead or follow? Conform or rebel? Give help or receive help? Were those early groups led by functional, trustworthy adults, such that you could simply relax and be a child? Or did you try to make up for an adult's failings — perhaps taking on the role of protector?

Knowing which group roles you gravitate toward is useful. It's a bit like knowing your trigger signature. For instance, if you know you played a protector/rescuer role as a child, you can make it a point to notice if you are still doing this in adult groups, and whether this is your best, most authentic choice. I know one woman, for example, who has a habit of carefully watching the leader or facilitator of any group she's in — to see if this leader is providing a safe container: Does the leader emphasize confidentiality enough? Is the leader clear about boundaries and expectations? Does the leader handle people's tender emotions in a compassionate way? This sort of function can be truly helpful to the group. But for the person performing this role, it may indicate they are in a chronic semi-triggered state without realizing it. They may have learned to avoid their own vulnerable feelings by becoming the group protector.

Keep this in mind as you read this chapter, and see if you recognize any early group experiences that may have influenced you, including your early relationship to authority.

Relationships with Authority

I like to remind people that we all started out little and dependent in a world of big people. These people were the authorities — parents, grandparents, teachers, clergy, coaches. Pause now to remember the big people who influenced you as a child. Were they fair? Did they cope well with their own emotions? Did you trust them? How did you feel about yourself in their presence? Did they give good guidance? Did you feel acknowledged and valued by them? Did any of them use you or abuse you? Keep these things in mind as you read this section on leadership and authority. Remember that groups, like individuals, have both conscious and unconscious motives and behaviors. The way a group behaves with respect to leadership or authority is often confusing and difficult to see — because most people are not aware of what we might call "the group unconscious."

No matter what the setting of a group, whether it is a work

group, a learning group, a social group, a support group, or a group of strangers, someone has to take a leadership role to keep things on track. This could be a designated group leader, facilitator, teacher, or boss. In less formal groups, it could be anyone who knows how to lead or take initiative. Once a leader is identified (even an informal leader), this person becomes a projection screen. Members will project their unmet childhood needs and unfinished emotional business onto the leader. Some members will give away their power to this person. Others will try to wrest power away from this person. Members may become very vigilant about what behavior this person rewards and what they punish or ignore. They may hold the person to an unrealistically high standard. Attitudes toward a group leader (including a nonleader who takes initiative) will vary — depending on what that person triggers in each person. This may have a lot more to do with each person's triggers than with the leader's skill or personality.

Recall a Triggering Event in a Group

See if you can recall an adult group experience when you got triggered by the leader or a group member. Can you bring back the details of this incident? What was the triggering event or stimulus? What was your reactive feeling, body sensation, and fear-story? Did you have an overt reaction — one that other group members could observe? Or was your reaction solely internal, such as silently judging the leader? Recall as much as you can, and go slowly through this memory. Then notice: How do you feel now as you replay the scene in your mind with your observing self actively witnessing? Be with this for a while. Notice if your triggered self was worried about how you were being seen or whether you were being judged. Was your triggered self worried more about other group members' opinions or the leader's? At the time when you were triggered, did you blame anyone? Did you expect the leader to do more to protect you?

Expecting a group leader to protect us (based on a fear of being unprotected) is an extremely common trigger. This may not even be what triggered us in the first place, but when a core fear gets triggered in a group (like a fear of being rejected or controlled), then we get to witness an additional layer of our trigger signature — feeling let down, betrayed, and disappointed by the person who was supposed to take care of us. If you recognize this as one of your triggers, pause now to acknowledge that you carry some vulnerability around being let down by someone in authority. See if you can feel empathy for the part of you who sometimes feels unprotected or not taken care of. If you expand your breathing to make space for this, maybe an old memory will surface. Don't work too hard to recall a memory. A memory will arise if your system is ready for it. If an old memory does arise, trust your own inner rhythm of *zooming in* (to see the memory up close) and *zooming out* (to view the memory from a distance) as you connect with it. What does this memory show you about your predisposition to feeling safe versus unsafe in groups?

When You're Triggered by Peers

In early school classes, as well as in families with more than one child, comparison and competition are common. Adults unwittingly foster insecurity in their children by making out-loud comparisons between them. A lot of trigger reactions relate to unfortunate early experiences where we were, or thought we were, being compared to someone else. Do you recall any painful experiences where this sort of thing occurred? Or maybe a parent did things to set you and a sibling or cousin up against each other. If this happened in your family, you might be especially sensitive to this sort of thing in peer-group situations. Expect to get triggered. And be ready to pause or mark a boundary at the first sign of triggering (see "Pausing in a Group," pages 183–85).

Comparing ourselves to others and being competitive are only two possible signs of reactivity. There are so many ways we can get triggered in a group. It is also possible to get triggered only in certain types of groups — for example, groups over a certain size, groups where we are expected to verbally share with everyone, or groups whose task involves something we're not good at, like public speaking. It's good to know which types of things might trigger you, so you can enter such a group with an extra degree of mindfulness.

If you are really astute, you may notice that you tend to get triggered most during a certain stage of a group's life, whether that's the beginning, middle, or final stages. Some are more anxious about beginnings. Others about endings. People who get triggered early on tend to have fears about trust, belonging, and dependency: *Can I trust this group or the leader? Do I belong? Do I have anything in common with these people? Do I feel included and significant versus invisible or ignored? Will I be protected?*

People who get triggered toward the middle stages of a group often fear that their unique voice or way of being will not be accepted. They worry about whether there will be enough airtime for them to be heard. They may watch the clock to see if some members get a longer turn to talk than they get. They may notice other group dynamics, such as if the men are doing all the talking and the women are mostly silent. People in this category often mistrust authority. They often get triggered by the designated leader or by any group member who asserts leadership or initiative. They may fear that if another group member takes control, this diminishes them — as if it shows weakness to be a follower.

People who get triggered toward the final stages of the group (in groups with a definite ending) tend to have triggers related to loss of connection, abandonment, or being alone. These are also the members who, at the final meeting of the group, will suggest that everyone stay in touch or perhaps have a reunion in six months. Having a certain type of trigger, such as abandonment, can lead someone to develop certain predictable personality patterns designed to manage this fear. I call these *control patterns* (which I discuss extensively in my other books). A control pattern is a personality habit (usually unconscious, not from choice) that functions to stave off the experience of being triggered. So if you have a fear of abandonment, you may try to organize a group reunion for a future date so you'll know that the last group session is not a final goodbye.

Pausing in a Group

Some group leaders may be sophisticated enough to introduce the idea of the pause agreement at the beginning of a new group. Most will not. If you have enough confidence, consider proposing this as a member. A pause agreement in a group is similar to the one used in a couple or friend relationship: If anyone notices themselves getting triggered, they say the word "pause," or use some other pause signal, and everyone stops talking and practices some form of self-calming or grounding for a minute or two. After the pause, the group will resume whatever it was doing, including sharing feelings and self-talk if this is part of the group contract. After a pause, the person who got triggered may not be ready for the group's attention right away, so they will need to communicate this, asking the group to carry on while they continue to practice self-calming.

In groups, reactivity often goes on for a while, and most of the group members can become triggered without necessarily being conscious of it. Witnessing two other group members in a heated conflict can be triggering for the whole group because members become "wired together" similar to couples. The group has a shared reality and a shared destiny, and its functionality affects everyone. If two group members (or two subgroups) are at odds, this affects everyone's ability to get their needs met. The same is true of a couple system, a family system, an organizational system, a governance system, and even a planetary system. Keep this in mind so you can become a more astute observer and a responsible participant in the systems you belong to.

It's impossible to prepare for every possible group situation, but here are a few more suggestions for what to do when you need a pause: If you're just beginning to get uncomfortable, and you're not yet triggered, you can slow things down by saying, "I need a few minutes to think about that." If you are already triggered, and you don't want to disrupt the group, you might say, "I'm taking a brief break, but I'll be back." If you need someone to quickly back off, and they have no sophistication regarding the concept of triggers or the idea of pausing, you may need to say something stronger, like "I want to hear what you're saying, but I'm getting upset. I need a break to calm myself." In all these examples, because the speaker is communicating responsibly and not blaming anyone, these statements are likely to be met with acceptance.

Marking Boundaries in a Group

In newer groups, clear norms and boundaries have not been established yet. The leader may suggest some ground rules to support safety, honesty, and responsible communication, but it can take a while before members consistently apply these guidelines. Even with the clearest and best guidelines, groups of people are unpredictable. Anyone might say anything at any given moment. And we could get triggered. We cannot prevent unwanted surprises.

What we can do is ask the group in advance to respect a particular boundary, one related to our triggers or trauma. We could ask, for example, that people refrain from certain behaviors or language, such as entering without knocking, shouting up close, making sexual jokes, using profanity, or using racial or ethnic slurs. We can also specify what pronoun we prefer. Ideally, the leader would invite everyone in the group to request such things up front, but if not, we can interrupt the group's activity to make our request. If you do this, make sure you have already done the inner work to accept your triggers and know your trigger signature.

Making this request does not guarantee your boundaries won't get challenged, however. Be prepared to speak up as soon as you can if someone says something that threatens to retraumatize you. If you're already triggered, you'll need to pause first. This is often best handled by pausing silently by yourself versus calling for a group pause. However, if you're not triggered yet, but know it's likely, you could speak to the group and say something like "I need to mark a boundary here. I have a sensitivity to hearing about sexual violence, so I am going to exit for a while."

Most groups will respect requests like this, but perhaps not uniformly. In any group of diverse individuals, not everyone may be equally accepting of trigger sensitivities. I, personally, have great respect for people who take risks like this to ask for what they want, because this is how group cultures change for the better. When individuals speak up about their uniquely personal needs and boundaries, this is how a group learns to embrace more diversity, to be more responsive to differing needs.

Task or Work Groups

Social groups and groups devoted to personal growth often welcome discussions of personal boundaries and emotional sensitivities. But in most business or community settings, group norms usually do not encourage this much emotional self-disclosure. In one of these settings, if you get triggered or start to get retraumatized, you may need to take a bathroom break. Taking a silent pause in your seat can also work, unless you feel the need to be alone.

In general, the goal is to know and respect your own limits and to be prepared to assert your needs and boundaries anywhere and everywhere, even if this is not the norm for a particular group. The more you have done the work of self-acceptance and self-compassion, the more effective you will be at getting your voice heard when you make such requests. In doing so, you become an inspiration for others who are less courageous, showing them the way toward better self-care. Even if the norm in the group is "we don't talk about feelings," you don't always have to conform. For example, in one in-person group I was facilitating, one of the participants asked for what she considered to be "special treatment." She said: "I feel shy about asking for this, but I request that during sessions and during the breaks that you do not touch or hug or elbow bump me without asking. I carry some old trauma around my physical boundaries being violated against my will.... Thanks for listening, and I'm glad I felt comfortable enough here to say this." In this instance, the request was related to a childhood trauma in an obvious way, and group members were happy to comply.

In other instances, your own version of "special treatment" could be something unrelated to triggers or trauma, such as asking for more frequent bathroom breaks or asking that people speak more loudly so you can hear them. Even though these sorts of things don't seem connected to getting triggered, if you do not ask, you could find yourself getting triggered later on because the group is not attending to your needs.

Self-Inquiry in Groups

In most groups, the whole group is not going to stop what it's doing while you process your personal trigger reaction. The important thing is that you recognize you have been triggered (because you know your trigger signature and your reaction patterns related to groups). When you notice some aspect of your trigger signature, silently begin your pause practice, followed by holding a compassionate space for your feelings.

Support this with conscious, deep breathing. In a group, you might not be able to do much, if any, self-inquiry. You may need to put that on hold until you get home and are in a safe and quiet location. Then when you do get home (or to a quiet place), come back to being with your tender feelings. Spend some time attending to the feelings that were triggered in the meeting or group. This does not mean you should crank up these feelings or intensify them. Simply allow them, and watch them change, flow, expand, contract, or get stuck somewhere. Don't worry if you don't experience resolution or closure. Just being with yourself like this is valuable in itself.

Repair in Groups

If you "got into it" with someone after becoming triggered in a group, the whole group will have been affected. When this happens, it's a good idea to do some sort of public repair. The best option is doing this face-to-face (either in person or via video conferencing), but second best is to do this via a group text or email. After you have fully calmed yourself, have gotten over your fear-story or any blaming, and have successfully restored a sense of safety, then fill out your repair statement (as in chapter 6). Depending on the timing, your public repair might occur during that same meeting or you may have to wait until the next time this group meets. Most often, people wait till the next meeting. In that case, tell the group ahead of time that you'd like to put something on the agenda: You'd like to bring them up to date on the trigger incident that they witnessed last time. Then you could address the person you were in conflict with, or you could address the group as a whole.

You might not want to read your entire repair statement, so modify it to fit your situation.

Here are two examples of how you might modify the repair script. The first is addressed to the other person involved in the incident:

"I'd like to apologize for what I said last week to you, Viv. I realized later I was triggered, so I was not thinking straight. I'm sorry. You didn't deserve that. I wish I could take it back."

Here's a different example addressed to the whole group:

"I want to bring you up to date on where I went with the anger I expressed last week about the new vacation schedule. After thinking about it, I see I was triggered. I have a history of getting triggered when something seems unfair. I'm sorry I reacted that way. If I could do it over, I would tell you, 'I'm feeling resistance to this plan and would like a day or two to think about it before voting on it.'"

You'll notice that these examples do not include a request for reassurance. Instead, I suggest using the sentence stem, "If I could do it over…," or the statement, "I wish I could take it back." I think the request for reassurance is only appropriate if you and the other person have a prior agreement to use your relationship as a path to healing and growth. Most groups do not have this sort of prior agreement — or at least most workplace groups don't.

However, whatever groups you are part of, once you know about triggering and have learned these trigger-work tools, I urge you to take the initiative to introduce these practices to the rest of your world. The world needs more people who know how to self-regulate, self-support, and be self-responsible. When you take the lead, others often appreciate it.

Chapter Eleven

I'm Leading a Group,
and Someone Gets Triggered

*People are going to get triggered in the groups
you lead. How prepared are you to address this
skillfully?*

If you lead or facilitate business meetings, personal development groups, community or church groups, or if you teach
in a school or college setting, you want the people in your
group to feel safe enough to bring their best resources and
attention. When people don't feel reasonably safe, the group
won't operate at its full potential. And if one person gets vis-
ibly triggered, this affects the whole group. Until this person
regains a sense of safety or equanimity, the whole group will
sense that something is off. It is your job to be aware of such
things.

You probably know by now that the world is full of people
who do not feel emotionally safe in general — whether they
appear to be triggered or not. Some of these people are going

191

to show up in your groups. For such people, being in a group will make them even more susceptible to getting triggered. I often observe out loud to my audiences that almost everyone seems to experience an increase in their social anxiety when they enter a group, especially a new group. After I say this, most audience members nod in agreement, as if they recognize themselves. Do you think this is true of you? If so, this can be an asset. It may be easier for you to spot subtle shifts in the mood of the group because your nervous system is more primed to notice this sort of thing. If not, that shouldn't be a problem as long as you know what to watch for. That's what this chapter is about.

Task Groups Versus Process Groups

Nowadays, even in business or community settings, most people have heard of getting triggered or getting one's buttons pushed. I started speaking and writing on this topic back in the early 1980s, when the concept was pretty new. Since then, the topic has gotten a lot more attention. Now, even in a work setting, it is not unheard of for group leaders to bring in some of the tools in this chapter. Most of these leadership practices are useful for both work and personal development settings, but you will need to adapt them to suit your particular context.

In personal development settings, leaders will often start right out acknowledging triggers and suggesting ground rules for how to manage them as part of setting the group context (see "Leadership Practices and Interventions," pages 202–8).

In work groups, this is generally not the norm. But once you get skilled at working with your own triggers, you may find it useful to take some risks in a business meeting — such as introducing ideas like a group pause or a post-group debriefing or repair. The more you have worked with these practices yourself, the more prepared you will be to adapt these tools to fit your group's needs and culture.

Leader Preparation

People are going to get triggered in the groups you lead. How prepared are you to address this skillfully? If you have worked with your own triggers, and integrated the Five Steps of Trigger Work, this is a good start: You accept that triggering happens; you know your unique trigger signature; you regularly practice pausing, self-regulating, and Compassionate Self-Inquiry; and you repair as needed and can stick to a simple repair script versus using repair as a time to defend your position, be heard, or explain your good intentions. By doing all these things, you embody an accepting, openhearted, and spacious attitude toward triggers. This attitude will get subtly communicated to the group. Your wise perspective will influence the group culture. If you are trying to teach this stuff, but you really think being triggered is something a leader needs to hide, then the group will pick up this attitude. This can influence members to try to deny or cover up their trigger reactions, but in doing so, their higher brain capacities will still be offline, so their ability to communicate, solve problems, and cooperate will be compromised.

Probably the most important thing for a leader to know is what their own trigger sensitivities are — because if they get triggered and continue to react unconsciously from that triggered place, group members are going to lose trust in them very quickly. This doesn't mean leaders cannot regain the group's trust with a skillful repair. But the goal is to notice trigger reactions right away before going too far into a reactive pattern.

Exercise: Recognizing Triggers as a Leader

Here's an exercise to help you recognize any triggers related to leadership:

Think of a time when you were in a leadership role and got triggered by a group member's behavior. What was the other person's behavior? What did you feel and sense? What was your reactive story, the meaning you gave to their behavior? What was your reactive behavior?

As you go back into the story and the fears associated with it, do you recognize a familiar theme? Does anything remind you of an earlier time in your life or an earlier painful experience in a group?

How do you feel as you notice your earlier self (or your pained or sensitive part) having this experience?

Do this exercise over and over as a way to get really good at spotting your leadership-related triggers. Once you're good at this, you'll be able to handle getting triggered as the leader of a group in a way that is not disruptive to the group. That is the goal. Until you get there, you might choose to actively call for a pause when you get triggered as the leader, and also request that everyone pause silently with you while attending to their own breathing and body sensations. At the end of the pause, if you are leading a personal development group, you might invite members to share what came up for them, either when asked to pause or during the pause. Did they find the pause helpful? Were they able to use the time to self-regulate? Did fear-stories, thoughts, or memories come up? If you're in a business meeting, you could facilitate this same type of sharing. Or you could say something like "Okay, I needed to get centered. Are we ready to get back to the agenda now?" For more on setting context and group expectations, including pausing when triggered, see "Leadership Practices and Interventions" (pages 202–8).

Frequent Triggers in Group Settings

As I've noted, being in a group will often automatically challenge many members' sense of safety. For one thing, it is harder to ask for what you want from a group of people versus one person. Further, some people have authority issues. Some people will instinctively become competitive with the leader or with other members. Some will spend a lot of mental energy comparing themselves to others in terms of appearance, intelligence, status, or personal power. Some personality types have core fears about visibility versus invisibility, some about autonomy versus conformity, and some about connection versus isolation. Here is a list of the most common issues and incidents that trigger people in groups, plus suggestions for what leaders can do. Remember, anything a leader can do can also be done by a courageous group member.

Criticism

As an example, let's say member A uses critical, blaming, or judgmental language toward member B. Member B gets their "fear of being blamed" or "fear of being criticized" button pushed. As the leader, you can facilitate group well-being by being on the lookout for signs of triggering whenever one member judges or criticizes another member and then doing one or more of the following: Call for a group pause; do "rounds" (a group awareness practice where each person says one word to describe their current feeling state; see "Other Helpful Devices," pages 206–8); share your own care, empathy, or other feelings for member B; and/or share your own care, empathy, or other feelings for member A.

Interpretation

Triggering can occur when member A refers to something member B has said, but inserts an interpretation or assumption about what was said that seems untrue to member B. Member B gets their "fear of being misunderstood" or "fear of not being seen" button pushed. As the leader, you can facilitate group well-being by being on the lookout for signs of triggering whenever one member makes an interpretation about another member, and then do one or more of the following: call for a group pause; share your own feelings, care, or empathy for member B; and/or share your own care, empathy, or other feelings for member A.

Plop

Member A offers what they think is a helpful comment or idea. No one responds to this contribution. It "plops." The person gets their "fear of being invisible" or "fear my voice doesn't matter" button pushed. If this happens, the leader might ask member A how they are feeling; share with member

A what they noticed and what they imagine — as in, "I noticed there was silence after you said what you want from the group, and I imagine you may be feeling something now. Are you?" — and/or share their own care, empathy, or other feelings for member A.

Time Scarcity

In a group where everyone is asked to share or weigh in on an idea, not everyone may speak up by the time the meeting is about to end. One member may think, *Time is running out, and my turn will be very short, if I even get a turn at all.* This member may get their "fear of not being important" or "fear of being left out" button pushed. As the leader, pay attention to the clock, and as time is getting short, mention this, and ask if anyone is sitting on any feelings about this.

Suggestion

Leaders often make comments, suggestions, or teaching points to individual members of the group. But if someone is especially sensitive to criticism and vigilant about whether leaders can hold a safe container, this person may get triggered based on their reactive story that the leader is harsh, critical, or insensitive. By the way, being a projection screen for members' core fears is an occupational hazard of a leader's job. If you get triggered by this, then this will be your "work" for a while, which means getting comfortable admitting you're triggered, initiating a group pause, and repairing as necessary.

In addition, other members might get triggered just witnessing a leader giving suggestions to someone else. Sometimes the person the leader talks to doesn't get triggered, but others do. It's as if some people are constantly watching the leader to see if they are holding a safe-enough container. A simple teaching point may be received by some members as a criticism, a put-down, or as taking a superior posture.

As the leader, be alert for subtle signs of reactivity after you offer suggestions or advice, but remember that you cannot avoid pushing some people's buttons. If you find that your behavior has triggered someone, take ownership for any unskillful behavior that you can own and perhaps tell the group, "If I could do it over, I would...."

Performance Anxiety

Say member A is invited to speak (or it's their turn in the circle), but they are unable to speak coherently. They have a freeze reaction. Words come out, but they don't make sense. The person is triggered by being on the spot or in the position of having to perform in front of others. Many people get a bad case of performance anxiety when speaking to more than two or three people. This might be a trigger reaction originating from early childhood experiences in school or other groups where the person experienced pressure to do things right (or failed to do something right).

As the leader, notice if you experience any impatience or frustration and give yourself a quick dose of self-soothing. You might reveal to the group an instance where you yourself got tongue-tied or experienced performance anxiety in a group. You can also invite the group to pause and self-calm, after which you might invite member A to have a do-over if they wish, or you might ask member A if they would like feedback from others about the impact of their behavior. However, do not allow others to give feedback to this person unless the person says they want feedback.

Group or Personal Identity

Sometimes, someone in the group may use a label or term when referring to someone else's gender, race, sexual orientation, or ethnicity, and one or more others in the group may judge this to be insensitive or inappropriate. These people may get triggered based on a fear-story that the person who spoke is unsafe, disrespectful, or disapproving. As the leader, be on the lookout for signs of triggering any time a member uses labels or terms that others might find upsetting or offensive, whether the terms are commonly regarded as inappropriate or not. If you notice someone is triggered, you might call for a group pause; do "rounds"; share your own care, empathy, or other feelings for whoever is upset; and/or share your care, empathy, or other feelings for the person who spoke.

Shame

Say a leader expresses anger or marks a boundary with a member publicly, or perhaps the leader simply corrects or offers advice to this member. This may trigger the member's fear of being publicly shamed. Perhaps this member has a history of shame-related trauma, and flooding or dissociation occurs. As the leader, be alert for signs of reactivity in such situations. When something you say triggers someone, take ownership for any unskillful behavior that you can own and perhaps tell the group, "If I could do it over, I would...." You may also want to apologize and reveal that you were triggered (if this is true).

Conflict

Conflict between two members, or any number of members, may trigger or retraumatize members who grew up in families where there was a lot of fighting or where there was addiction, mental illness, or lifestyle instability. For such group members, unresolved conflict situations can trigger fears of conflict or chaos.

As the leader, be alert for signs of reactivity whenever there is conflict in a group. Invite a group pause, saying something like "Sometimes when there is conflict in a group, this can be upsetting, and not just for the people involved in the interaction. I suggest we all take a moment to connect with ourselves and calm our nervous systems together. Will you join me by closing your eyes and taking four or five slow full breaths?" After the pause, you might invite sharing regarding how people reacted to the conflict, what this brought up for them, and/or how they are feeling now in their bodies. This might also be a good time to do "rounds."

Overwhelm

When group members are giving feedback to an individual, this individual may become overwhelmed and be unable to mark a boundary and ask to be left alone. Other members may notice this but not feel empowered to speak up. If the leader does not recognize this, and others do, some group members may judge the leader as incompetent.

As the leader, be alert to overwhelm in group members. If you ever realize you have failed to address this, do a personal inquiry involving self-compassion, and take responsibility for any sensitivities, fears, and blind spots you encounter in doing this inquiry. Publicly take ownership for any unskillful behavior that you can own, apologize, or make a public statement to the group, "If I could do it over, I would. ..." Make note of what you have learned going through this painful experience, and appreciate yourself for being open to feedback and continuous learning.

Addressing Other Triggers

In addition to this list, group members will possess or exhibit many other trigger sensitivities as well. Group members bring with them the ghosts from their past that they have unfinished emotional business with. It's not just the leader who is a projection screen. It's also the group itself.

It's impossible to anticipate every potential situation. Just remain alert for trigger reactions, call for a group pause when you're in doubt, and be open to input and advice from group members. To be healthy, a group needs to have the capacity to learn and grow together. The leader does not need to have all the answers. The leader's job is to facilitate group development and learning, to facilitate cooperation toward a common goal, and to help members find ways to use their unique gifts and resources to further these aims. Sometimes these aims are best served when leaders adopt a not-knowing posture and remain open to learning with and from others as everyone goes through a challenging situation together.

If you make an error in judgment, it's important to own up to this immediately and do a public repair. People tend to be pretty forgiving when leaders open up and admit a mistake — as long as leaders do not defend themselves while doing so. Defensiveness erases an otherwise sincere apology.

Apologize first to those who were hurt by your actions. Then, when triggers have been calmed (yours especially), ask if people are willing to hear your explanation or perspective on the situation. Do not assume the answer will be yes. Watch everyone's response carefully, and if people are not yet ready to listen openly to your side of the story, do not proceed. Bring the matter up again at a later time.

Leadership Practices and Interventions

This section describes some useful group leadership practices for minimizing, managing, and working skillfully with trigger reactions in groups.

Setting Context: Purpose, Ground Rules, and the Leader's Role

When a group first starts, or when joining an existing group as the new leader, share your sense of the group's purpose, ground rules for communicating, and your perspective on your role. Then share some of your values about what fosters group health and safety and your expectations of conduct. In a personal development context, this might include values like respect for differences, openhearted listening, honesty, risk taking, balanced participation, and taking responsibility for one's own reactions. In a work context, you might emphasize values like openness to learning and feedback, willingness to ask for help, sharing information, and taking initiative.

Explain how you see your role and leadership style. Are you more directive or laissez-faire? Are you the person to go to if people have problems with another member, or do you expect members to work things out among themselves? Do you call on people to make sure everyone's voice is heard, or do you leave that up to each individual? If you are playing the dual role of both leader/facilitator and group member, how will you let everyone know when you are speaking as a member versus as the boss, leader, teacher, trainer, or expert? For instance, some facilitators/teachers will literally change hats; some wear beads when they are being the teacher.

In my personal development groups, I let members know that in my role as teacher, I will be interrupting them sometimes to help them notice the feelings or assumptions underneath their stated message, or to help them notice their trigger sensitivities or unconscious communication habits. I need to get their consent on this so they will not be shocked or insulted when this happens. Despite this, some will still get triggered by being interrupted. But in my groups, this is grist for the learning mill. After I interrupt, I watch for signs of triggering.

Some groups start off getting group agreement to use mutually developed communication guidelines, which might include the following: no interrupting, making I-statements, keeping shares under one minute, and accepting the fact that members might get triggered or feel overwhelmed at times.

Whether you have such guidelines or not, it is still a good idea to acknowledge that triggering may happen and to get agreement about what to do when it does. You might start this discussion by mentioning that things can get going pretty fast sometimes, resulting in some members' feeling left out or left behind. Or things can get said in the heat of the moment that come across to some as disrespectful or insulting. Things like this may bring on trigger reactions, both hidden and overt. Then introduce the idea of the group pause: If anyone feels stressed or triggered or thinks someone else might be — whether this seems obvious or not — they say the word "pause" or "time-out" or some other easy-to-remember signal. Some groups have a nonverbal hand-raising signal or a bell or chime for this purpose. If anyone gives this signal, everyone stops talking and brings their attention inward to their body sensations and breathing, with the aim of becoming more relaxed, grounded, and present. If you wish, explain that the ability to self-regulate is necessary for most group endeavors, whether the endeavor is a design problem or an intimacy game. Also add that in groups, if one member gets triggered, other members will sense this and they may become triggered themselves, or at least distracted. The reason for becoming aware of triggers and pausing is so that all members can be mentally present for the task at hand. When there is unacknowledged triggering going on, communication can become untrustworthy.

The method I use when I lead Honesty Salons — which focus on communicating with self-awareness — is to give everyone in the group a four-inch round toy button. I tell them, "We all have buttons, or the potential for getting our buttons pushed." One of my goals is to help people accept this fact with more ease, tenderness, self-compassion, and humor. Then I explain: "If you get your button pushed or become triggered during the group, hold up your toy button so everyone can see it. Then we will all take a brief pause for four or five slow, deep breaths. During this pause, each of us should notice if we ourselves are also triggered or in need of a pause." Any item, such as a pen, can also be used as a signal.

How to Facilitate a Group Pause

There are different ways to deal with trigger reactions, depending on the setting, the leadership model you are using, the group purpose, and the group's stage of development. But if you have put in place an explicit pause agreement with a group, your job will be easier. Here are two common scenarios and how to handle them: first when someone is triggered and asks for a pause, and second when someone is triggered but doesn't say anything.

If a member gets triggered and says "pause," make sure everyone is quiet for four to ten breaths. After the silence, invite some general group sharing about how each person is feeling. This sharing is aimed at the group, not at the person who said "pause," and it is not meant as an invitation to discuss what happened, but simply a quick indication of each member's current state. This is similar to doing rounds (see "Other Helpful Devices" below).

Then ask the person who said "pause" if they need anything, or if they would prefer that the group move on so they can do some inner inquiry or self-soothing on their own. In general, as a group leader, I do not usually help the person process their trigger reaction in the group unless the group is explicitly a personal growth workshop where this is part of the contract. When I do choose to help the person, I guide them in the Compassionate Self-Inquiry practice, often inviting everyone else in the group to do their own inquiry silently. However, whether you decide to spend group time helping the triggered person get calm and clear or not, at some point you need to move the group's attention away from this person. At an appropriate moment, ask if everyone is ready to move on, and if they are, tell those who might have more to share that they can do so later. Then provide time at the end of the meeting for debriefing, closure, revising, or repairing with those who want this, using whatever terms are appropriate for your aims and the group culture.

In the second common scenario, a member will get triggered, shut down or freeze, and no one will call for a pause. The moment you notice someone is triggered, say something to normalize or show acceptance for their reaction, such as, "It is understandable that some people might be triggered hearing this," or "I believe there are some trigger reactions in the room." Then call for a group pause, and maybe guide a brief self-calming or self-compassion practice — modified to fit your group's needs and norms. After this, invite general group sharing as above — using whichever tools are appropriate for your situation.

Other Helpful Devices

Here are some other helpful devices for groups. These devices enhance everyone's ability to be present, authentic, or self-aware. When members are aware and present, the group will experience less frustration and fewer triggering episodes.

I Feel / Period Cards: A device I use in the Honesty Salon is to give everyone an 8.5-by-11-inch card. One side of the card has the phrase "I feel..." and the other side has the word "Period." The "I feel..." side of the card is used when a person is talking, and someone else in the group thinks the talker may have gone away from their present felt experience and begun intellectualizing, generalizing, or rehashing a familiar story. The listener then holds up the "I feel..." sign so the person talking can see it. This prompts the talker to check in with themselves to notice feelings and body sensations before continuing to speak. Once in a while the talker will get triggered when seeing the "I feel..." sign, but in my groups, triggering is an opportunity for inquiry, not something to avoid.

The side of the card that says "Period." is used if a listener thinks the talker is starting to go into an unconscious pattern of repeating or overexplaining. The listener will hold up the "Period." sign. This prompts the talker to pause momentarily to notice if they have made their point, if they feel complete, if they feel anxiety about ending their sharing, and so on. I think many members tend to talk on and on because they feel anxiety about how they are being received by their listeners. They fear they aren't clear or that they might be argued with, so they keep talking, trying to find a more clear, or unarguable, way to say what they mean. Members of my groups have told me that using this "Period." sign has helped them become more self-aware in other groups they belong to. They notice their tendency to overexplain and often find themselves silently saying "period" to themselves, usually with an attitude of self-acceptance and humor.

Rounds: If your group seems to be stuck, or you're not sure if members are suppressing difficult feelings, atypical contributions, or trigger reactions, do rounds: Invite each member to speak one word into the group space that describes how they are feeling. In a large group video conferencing format, you might use the chat function — so participants write one word in the chat. This is a way to take the pulse of the group quickly. It also gives the whole group a snapshot of the group's mood. Leaders are often surprised by what gets revealed. As a leader, you may assume people are quiet because they don't feel safe, but after doing rounds, you might discover that there is a wide range of experiences among members with regard to how safe they feel. In my experience, a leader is not always able to assess the group mood. There is often more diversity of feelings and opinions than is apparent until you ask.

Categories Game: In a personal growth group or some training contexts, you can diagnose the probable level of emotional pain members are carrying by leading them in the categories game. This activity also demonstrates to everyone how their feelings and life experiences compare with others in the group.

The game is simple. Have everyone stand in a circle, then name various categories of experience — like "anyone who has ever felt social anxiety in a group of more than four people" or "anyone who was raised in a single-parent home." Anyone who relates to or belongs in the category then steps into the center of the circle. (In a virtual meeting, have people raise their hands or use the hand-raising function.) Once in the center, pause for everyone to notice who includes themselves and who doesn't and to notice how they feel. Then people in the center return to the larger circle, and the leader announces another category. In this game, choose topics or issues that you think may reveal everyone's vulnerability to getting triggered. For example, you can name categories like "anyone who has a fear of being ignored," "anyone who fears being misunderstood," "anyone who fears being controlled," and so on. At some point, you can invite members to add their own categories, but they can only name ones that they themselves belong to. This exercise can bring people to a deep level of sharing very fast — depending on the categories. This activity also gives you a picture of how much vulnerability members are ready to reveal.

The Leader's Skill, Emotional Maturity, and Experience

A leader is always learning and getting better at this craft. Experience counts for a lot. But no matter how experienced you are, things may happen that require a level of skill above your pay grade. When triggering incidents go unnoticed and unprocessed, this can create weird group dynamics — hidden agendas, covert competitiveness or undercutting, outlandish projections, scapegoating, people withdrawing or staying silent, and so on. If a group goes through a cascade of unacknowledged triggering events, this can foster regression and chaos.

Members instinctively know when a group is operating in a healthy way. When it is not, certain members will act out the unconscious fears of the group — sometimes leading to a shared sense of unreality or chaos. If a group you are leading seems to be regressing in this way, that's a signal to take a step back and invite members to become group observers with you. Use your authority to bring the group's attention to what is happening here and now. You might suggest that everyone pause and step back with you, taking the posture of an observer of this group. Report what you are noticing and ask if others agree with you that something is off. Once this is established, make a clear leadership statement like "We cannot continue with our task until we sort this out, and I'm going to need your input. I request that we all consider together: What might be going on here? Do people feel safe? Do you think people feel valued? Are there any unresolved issues, unrepaired triggers, or conflicts from the past that might be creating mistrust? Is there anything that anyone has noticed or felt that might be useful here?"

The discussion that ensues may or may not solve the problem. But whether it solves the problem or not, it is still worth doing. Even if your efforts fail, and the group chaos continues, doing this is part of your learning and the group's learning. If you want to further enhance your learning, get some supervision from someone more experienced than yourself. Therapists get supervision when they need it. Group leaders need supervision, too.

Group Debriefing, Revising, and Repairing

There are several good ways to end a group where triggering has occurred. These may need to be integrated with the group's other closure rituals or practices, that is, with the things this group normally does when ending. One good way to assess the group's state of mind is to do rounds. Another is to ask a few specific questions about the triggering episode, such as the following, and request responses with a show of hands:

- How many are still feeling somewhat shaken by the interaction between _____ [whoever was involved]?
- How many are feeling the need to debrief today's meeting for a little while?
- How many are going to seek out someone here to talk to later about what happened in this group?
- How many got triggered during the group today? Of those people, how many are still carrying some sense of agitation or anxiety?

If two group members had a triggering conflict that everyone witnessed, you could guide the pair to fill out a repair statement (see chapter 6). Adjust the script for your purpose or situation, and perhaps simplify to only a few sentences, for example:

When I [saw, heard, did, said] _____, I was [or got] triggered. If I could do it over, I would tell you that my fear of _____ was triggered, and I need your help to feel _____.

Then invite the protagonists to read their filled-out scripts aloud to each other in front of the group. As the leader, you might need to help them find the right words to describe their experience, and they will probably need help sticking to the script. People unfamiliar with repair statements may revert to old communication habits, like trying to explain or defend themselves or telling others what they should have done. If this happens, you need to interrupt this — perhaps reminding everyone to use uncomplicated, vulnerable I-statements to avoid retriggering others.

After this, some or all of the other group members who got triggered would read their filled-out scripts, modifying the second sentence to read: "If I could do it over, I would acknowledge to myself that my fear of _____ was triggered, and that I need to feel _____." At the very end, encourage a few people to share their appreciations with others for something specific they have just witnessed.

Repair and Closure in Other Conflict Situations

As the leader, if you and a group member get into a conflict, you can use this same process for repair and closure: You both fill out a brief repair script and then read your scripts to each other with the group witnessing.

If the triggering incident involved one member pushing a lot of buttons in the room, this needs to be handled very carefully to prevent a pile-on or scapegoating. In this case, I suggest asking everyone to fill out a modified repair script, focusing on acknowledging to themselves their trigger reactions and sensitivities. An example might be: "When I heard you say 'not now,' I got triggered. It was probably my fear of rejection coming up. I need to feel valued and appreciated." Then end by acknowledging that the group has gone through a tough experience together and that the task now is for each person to consider what they have learned in order to be more resourceful and resilient in the future.

Some group incidents will leave hurts and fears unattended to — or only partially attended to. Closure is not always possible. If you think that some group members are walking away feeling upset, consider reaching out to them afterward to offer a private conversation. Choose the individuals you think are hurting the most or who may not have good self-regulation habits.

My personal philosophy is "we will all die with unfinished business." Not everything can be resolved to the satisfaction of all concerned. Life can be messy. Motivations are complex. In any situation, I am only one person. I cannot prevent every unfortunate outcome or make everyone happy. My job is to do the best I can in each situation that life presents. Sometimes I will fall short of what others expect of me. If there is any experience in my life that has helped me come to these conclusions, it is my experience leading groups!

Groups Are a Microcosm

I'd like to close this chapter by emphasizing the importance of helping people in your groups learn to *be with* emotional pain and interpersonal discomfort. As I see things, humanity's collective developmental task is to get better and better at seeing and dealing with inconvenient truths (from a dysfunctional marriage to the climate crisis) so we can make needed changes and continue to evolve. If we are going to make such changes and decisions cooperatively, we need to be able to communicate respectfully with people who see things very differently from ourselves. For this, we need to have all our higher brain resources online. Differences tend to push buttons, automatically diverting us into the reptilian part of our brains. It's too easy to fall into reactive patterns like blaming or projecting our disowned parts onto "the other." It's not easy to inquire deeply into our reactions and unfinished emotional business or to embrace our rejected or outcast parts.

Inner work in the company of others is a process of becoming whole. I call this "whole-making" — which means making ourselves more whole by discovering or reconnecting with our rejected parts. When we take on this work as a lifelong practice, we come to know and embody this whole-making process. This brings us to a perspective where we are no longer trying to solve problems "at the level of the problem" (that is, from the same level of consciousness where the problem was created). Our perspective and range of perceived options is no longer limited by the narrow self-interested agenda of avoiding emotional discomfort or trouble. That's the level of consciousness where the current problems were created. As a facilitator of wholeness, we are inspiring our group members to welcome inconvenient truths and painful challenges as opportunities for becoming more whole and refined human beings. Personal lessons, when shared publicly, contribute to everyone's learning and to the healing of the community. As we experience ourselves as participants in this whole-making process, we realize the inseparability of inner work (to reclaim our neglected parts) and *world work* (to create a world that works for everyone and every life-form).

Chapter Twelve

I'm Triggered
by the World Situation

True strength and wisdom, the kind that enable us to cope with the complexity of today's world situation, require integrated input from all parts of the system, including the vulnerable parts.

Our world is suffering from so many intersecting crises. We are acutely aware of the climate crisis, the unemployment crisis, the culture wars, the mental health crisis, the opioid epidemic, the homeless crisis, the refugee crisis, the hunger crisis, and the suicide crisis. Then there is the huge wealth gap, war or the threat of war, racism, climate migration, and the rise of fascism in many countries. In the United States, we see increasing polarization between political parties who advocate very different policies regarding the role of government in civil rights, public health, healthcare, birth control, race and gender equality, corporate power, food safety, environmental protection, education, and poverty. Just writing this paragraph, trying to use language that is as objective as possible, I can sense some agitation in my nervous system. The collective soup we all swim in is reaching the boiling point. And it is affecting everyone — some more than others, of course.

How often do you look at a news article or turn on the TV news and feel anger, frustration, helplessness, overwhelm, outrage, panic, depression, or fear? As the litany of seemingly unsolvable problems grows, more and more people are feeling stressed out. In 2020, the *Washington Post* reported that one-third of Americans experience frequent or chronic anxiety or depression. In that same year *Forbes* magazine printed a letter from an emergency medicine specialist in Los Angeles that stated, "Suicide hotline phone calls have increased 600%." The more stressed out we feel, the more triggerable we are. And the more easily we can be manipulated by special interest groups who seek to hijack our amygdala or take advantage of our dysregulated state to push their agendas. If we want to maintain a sense of equanimity and inner sovereignty in this chaotic world, we need good self-regulation habits.

Psychologists and many activists have found that effective action is the best antidote to anxiety and depression. But how can anyone act effectively when they are triggered? When we're triggered, we are disconnected from our higher brain's problem-solving capacities. We are unable to think clearly.

If we want to become part of the solution, instead of projecting our personal problems onto the collective heap, we need to learn how to separate our personal trigger reactions from what is actually going on. Once we get good at doing this, then we can use our personal feelings to fuel our genuine outrage, effective action, or sacred grief. That's what this chapter is about: how to use our emotional sensitivities as fuel for an effective and heartfelt response to any world problem, while at the same time having a well-regulated nervous system and differentiating our reactive behaviors and stories from what actually needs to change. To do good in the world, or just to sort out fact from fiction, we need to have sovereignty over our own inner state.

Using the World as a Doorway to Self-Knowledge

In my work, I spend a lot of time hearing about people's private fears and triggers. One coaching client, Rita, revealed how she got triggered whenever she read stories about political polarization in the United States. She also reacted when she heard newscasters, neighbors, and relatives using demeaning labels toward people on the other side of the political divide.

When Rita and I explored her reactive feelings, she connected emotionally to several early school experiences with peers when she was around ten or eleven. As a Mexican American, she was part of a minority group in her school. Kids that age can be cruel as they navigate the developmental task of discovering their personal power. Rita was teased and put down for being Mexican. As she remembered some childhood scenes, what hurt her most was the name-calling, the racial slurs. Through her inner work with me, she was able to use this as a doorway to deeper self-empathy and self-support. When she allowed herself to weep and feel the impact of these old hurts, with her inner witness engaged, she connected with a new resource within herself. Instead of judging her reactive feelings, she learned to listen to these feelings, to really attend to them, and to embrace them with the sort of compassion she would offer a much-loved child.

Before learning to do this, she would get totally overwhelmed, causing her to shut down and withdraw. Now she was willing to face the pain rather than hide from it. She gradually found herself taking on this issue as a cause among her community of friends and neighbors. Whenever someone used demeaning or snarky language toward people they disagreed with, she would speak up and share how this felt to her. She would say things like: "You know, I have been on the receiving end of a lot of insulting labels in my childhood, being Mexican in a mostly Anglo community, so it pains me when you talk this way. I'd rather hear something specific about your experience with this person — something they actually did or said and how that affected you. I really want to know what you think and feel. I just have trouble when I hear labels like 'crazy' or 'ignorant,' and I don't know what they did that you're referring to ... or why this bothers you."

I think Rita's story illustrates how helpful it can be to get to the bottom of our trigger reaction, so we can use what's happening in the world around us as a doorway to deeper self-knowledge, self-compassion, and community action. Perhaps even more important is how, after she learned to feel her hurt rather than deny it, Rita became less self-righteous toward friends and neighbors who triggered her. Instead of shutting down and gossiping to others, she felt empowered and emboldened to speak up. In her own way and in her own social circles, she became a leader and a champion for constructive political discourse — for a way of conversing that relies on sharing real data about what really happened and does not resort to name-calling, innuendos, and put-downs. Through doing her trigger work, Rita connected with the source of her own passion for this issue — which made her leadership efforts all the more compelling and effective.

Civil Disobedience

When deep structural change is needed in a society, and those in power deny basic human rights to certain segments of the population, civil disobedience, or taking it to the streets, may be the only remaining option. The type of trauma response that occurs when a person is without food, shelter, a sustainable future, and physical safety is quite different from the attachment traumas I discuss in this book. But a person's ability to sort out unproductive responses to unjust authority from more clearheaded responses is still worth attending to.

Rita's story illustrates how we need to be mindful of how we can sabotage our own credibility when we throw around inflammatory verbiage, negative labels, and vague generalizations. I believe we can speak with passion without sacrificing critical thinking. We can make a righteous point without being self-righteous. We can use anger to assert that something needs to stop without becoming so angry that we become wrongheaded or trigger others into dangerous behavior. If we do the inner work suggested in this book, we will notice when we are becoming wrongheaded, inflammatory, self-righteous, or needlessly repetitive. If we are called to lead or organize any sort of civil disobedience action, then we must use the tools of any good leader. Much of our power is in the legitimacy of our words, the sincerity in our call to action, our ability to paint a clear picture with our words, and to point out realistic options (rather than speaking from reactivity and fomenting chaos). We must use our voice wisely.

Remember, a good leader's actions promote "the good of the whole." We may be advocating a change to rebalance power or resources. But our ultimate aim is to have the whole system work more effectively — for everyone. The ability to hold this whole-systems perspective will be challenged by people who do not understand the holistic interrelatedness of all parts of the system — that we're all in this together. These parties may advocate for division — divide and conquer, characterizing issues as us against them. They may try to keep our amygdala activated as a power play — because they know this makes people less effective. Such divisive tactics are never an effective long-term strategy.

If we have done our inner trigger work, we will be less susceptible to this sort of manipulation and mind control. When we have sovereignty over our own nervous system, devious characters cannot hijack our brain for their agendas. And we will understand in our bones this whole-making process because we have learned to balance our own internal system of subparts, allowing our neglected parts to be seen, heard, accepted, and loved. When we embody this level of whole-system awareness, our actions are more likely to be aligned with the laws of how the universe actually works. We know that when a system takes everyone's needs into account, there is less reason to fear one another. Fearing one another can lead to conflict and chaos. We come to understand this by seeing what fear does inside our nervous system. The mark of a healthy human system — whether it be a person, a couple, or a country — is good, well-regulated communication between subparts. This allows us to make good decisions. Our parts cannot hear one another when our survival alarms are ringing.

How Inner Work Supports Outer Work

Another story from a client, Jim, illustrates how inner work can help us cope with being triggered by tragic world news, political turmoil, economic downturns, social injustice, and other difficult events.

During the 2020 coronavirus pandemic, Jim became overwhelmed by both his family's circumstances and the US government's response to the economic downturn. Jim's adult kids were out of work, and he was not even sure about the security of his own employment. When he read about federal contracts and economic aid being disproportionately awarded to large companies with political connections, while small businesses like his were being overlooked, he became angry. This felt deeply unfair to Jim, who always proudly stood up for fairness and justice. In fact, he sometimes expressed his outrage over social injustices so aggressively that his friends would tell him, "I can't discuss this with you anymore." This time, Jim's trigger reaction was so strong he could not find words to express himself. He felt overwhelmed and helpless, nearly paralyzed. When he was not at his job, all he wanted to do was distract himself with food and screen time.

Jim decided to do the Compassionate Self-Inquiry practice, beginning with the very heavy feeling he sensed in his chest and torso when he thought of this recent injustice. He started by closing his eyes and paying attention to his breathing. When relaxed, he was able to activate the innate curiosity of his witnessing self, allowing a bifurcation in his way of experiencing all this — so he experienced himself as both *the witness* and *the one being witnessed*. Then he came back to noticing the body sensation of heaviness, allowing this to be there, as he breathed fully and deeply to open up inner space for what might arise. From this more spacious inner presence, he observed the heaviness becoming more contracted, tighter. He remained curious and welcoming. Soon, he noticed that the sensations were starting to feel overwhelming, so he opened his eyes and looked around the room for a minute. He stood up and shook his arms a few times before closing his eyes again and resuming the inquiry. As he watched his feelings and sensations move and change, he suddenly felt very afraid. He remembered to keep breathing slowly and fully as a childhood memory emerged. In the memory, Jim was about seven years old. Something was happening in the next room that felt violent and out of control. He heard loud voices. He opened the door and saw his father throwing a chair at his mother as his older sister tried to intervene. His little boy body seemed paralyzed, like he couldn't move. His voice was so constricted that no sound came out when he tried to speak. Little Jim retreated to his bedroom and hid under the covers, feeling helpless and numb.

As Jim connected on a feeling level with the terror of this traumatic memory, he was also witnessing it with tenderness. His witnessing self was able to hold space for the terror with compassion. He remembered to keep breathing fully. Tears came, and he sobbed for a little while, allowing his body to shake and tremble. Pretty soon, as the tears subsided, he realized these were tears of grief — grief over what that little boy had to deal with at such a young age, grief over how his conditioning had taught him to fear conflict rather than showing him how to deal with it in a balanced way. His approach to conflict had always been to either dominate or submit — nothing in between. When people approach interpersonal conflicts in this way, it means they are triggered.

Jim sat with his sadness, grief, and tenderness, allowing the different pieces of this experience to fall together, until he felt, at once, both relaxed and somewhat energized. He noticed his breathing became calm and steady. His chest and torso area felt light and expanded. It was as if a weight had lifted, and he could move and breathe more freely.

After going through this process, Jim told me he experienced more self-trust and inner calmness. He was pretty sure he would get triggered again by incidents of injustice, and he was open to continuing his self-examination around the issue. When he reflected on his adult reaction to issues of fairness and justice, he recognized that he had a pattern of "either seeing red or shutting down." His reactions to the injustices around him exhibited either too much or not enough force. But when he heard himself using the word "force," this caught his attention. He began to pay more attention to how he dealt with conflicts around fairness in his daily life, asking himself: Do I trust myself only when I feel "forceful" and sure of myself, when I know I have the upper hand? Am I so overwhelmed by the complexity of today's world predicament that I can't feel forceful anymore? Is this why I hold back, and why I feel so passive and lethargic? Have I lost my ability to speak up?

As he reflected on his relationship to the unjust authority in his own family of origin (represented by his father), he realized how powerless he had always felt as a child. His dad would often blow up at him when Jim had no idea what he had done or what his dad wanted him to do differently. This left him feeling frozen, not knowing what to do or say. As an adult, Jim thought he had overcome that childhood sense of "I'm not enough." He thought he had grown up into a man with "force" — a man who was bigger, more sure of himself, and more authoritative than his father. He could see now that this need to appear forceful had come at a price. He had developed a rigid, inflexible personality structure, what psychologists call an authoritarian personality. He had denied the part of himself that felt terrified by his dad's harsh criticism and aggression as well as the part that didn't know what to do. He had completely turned his back on that seven-year-old boy cowering under the bedcovers. When that part of him got triggered by an intense and complex world situation, one that was controlled by forceful, unyielding, and seemingly unfair authorities, he collapsed into lethargy.

Jim is still working to integrate these parts of his own psyche. Doing inner inquiry into his trigger reactions regarding unfairness has opened him up to fruitful self-questioning. He has found real value in pausing to be with his trigger reactions and connecting with a long-denied part of himself that fears feeling overwhelmed and powerless. Going forward, Jim's ability to temper his forcefulness with an awareness of this fearful aspect will help him learn to communicate his needs and values in a more balanced way — blending confidence with humility. He decided to join a men's group that focuses on sharing hidden feelings and shadow parts, and he is learning to admit when he needs help or guidance. His rigidities are relaxing as he feels safer not knowing. The men's group has been a good place to explore how the world situation is putting him in touch with previously denied fears and insecurities. He knows he is on a journey that never ends.

Triggering as a Wake-Up Call

Sometimes what we think is a bad thing turns out to be good for us. Sometimes we need something unpleasant to shock us into paying better attention to things we were not aware of. In my work with couples, I often see one or both partners recognizing that they needed to get whacked on the side of the head by some circumstance in their outer world (in this case, a difficult marriage) in order to pay attention to the need for inner change.

One client, Rachel, described having this realization as she explored her frustrations in her marriage. She reflected: "When I first started counseling, I thought I was with the wrong person. Like, why would I want to be with someone who upsets me so much, where I often feel so unloved and unprotected? But now I see that blaming him was not the answer. I am seeing that so many of my personality defense mechanisms and fear-stories were connected to unprocessed hurtful childhood experiences. I was going around so bound up, so defended, and not really feeling much of anything. There was this pain inside that I was completely unaware of, but my fear of feeling that pain was running me.

"Being married to Bob forced me to see how insecure I am, how I am always watching and waiting for someone to let me down. It would start with some careless action on his part, and I would think, *I don't matter to him, I'm invisible.* Then I would sense a tightening and clenching sensation in my chest. Through counseling, I learned to be with this sensation, to feel it, to be curious and see where this led me. It led me to uncover a part of myself that felt so alone as a kid, the ten-year-old kid my parents didn't have time for. They had show dogs, and the dogs got all their attention. Plus, by the time I got home from school, my mom would be drunk. I have recently learned to love and care for this lonely, hurting part of me. I am still grieving for what the younger me didn't get. But I feel stronger and better about myself. I am mostly happy with Bob now. I ask for what I want, so that helps. I used to just complain or go away."

In Rachel's case, her reaction to her husband woke her up to denied or neglected parts of herself, but the same thing can happen with our reaction to any external or world event. In my coaching practice, I see more and more situations where "what's going on" — from a corporation's tax evasion to a biased ruling from a judicial body — triggers people to become aware of their disowned shadow and their hidden pain.

What used to be hidden (unconscious) is becoming conscious. Consider these three examples:

One woman found herself getting triggered by former President Donald Trump whenever he would make demeaning public comments to reporters and officials who challenged him. When she went deeply into the feelings and memories that this triggered, she recalled forgotten events from her childhood, when she was abused and ridiculed by a narcissistic mother. As she was bringing compassion to the child part of her that carried a fear of being unlovable and worthless, a feeling of anger came up. As she explored this angry part, allowing this part to speak out against the abuse she had suffered, she realized that this anger represented her inner protector. This long-denied resource was the inner voice that says, "The way you are treating me is not okay, and it must stop." This part knew what she really needed and had the courage to express this. It was the voice inside that had been muffled by her fear of speaking up to her mother. After doing this inner work, she experienced a change in her relationships with men. As an adult, she had often been drawn to abusive relationships, but now she felt empowered to express her current needs and boundaries effectively, instead of being a doormat. She found her authentic voice rather than thinking she always had to adapt to others.

One man found himself getting triggered when he saw TV news depicting police brutality. Exploring his trigger reaction, he was able to own his grief about growing up with a some-times violent father. As a child, he never felt safe, and much of his energy and focus had been on protecting himself from physical harm. Doing Compassionate Self-Inquiry, he learned to use his reactions to seeing violence on TV as a chance to offer empathy to himself, reassuring his fearful part, the part he judged as weak, that fear is a normal, healthy reaction to threats of physical violence — especially if you are small and the other person is big. Accepting his fear allowed him to de-velop a more realistic assessment of which events in his life were actually dangerous, and which were not. Then he could take action as needed or let it go when there was no real threat.

One man found himself getting triggered during the Trump administration whenever Republican politicians would repeat or defend falsehoods being spread by the president. When he explored his trigger reaction, he recalled childhood incidents where his alcoholic father would berate and belittle him while his mother, the enabler in this instance, quietly watched. After he worked with these painful memories — embracing, own-ing, and integrating both his fearful part and his inner protec-tor — he was eventually able to clear the air with both of his parents before they died.

In all three cases, as the individuals continued the inner work that began with seeing themselves getting triggered by the world situation, they developed the ability to speak up more effectively with others to assert their needs and values, call out wrong behavior, or defend their beliefs.

Life Wants Us to Heal and Become Whole

As these stories show, sometimes we need to get our buttons pushed so we can see where we still have some inner healing to do, so we can learn to offer acceptance and love to our neglected parts. Emotional pain can open the door to healing and effective action. When we learn to be curious and open-hearted about our trigger reactions, allowing our attention to follow the painful or upset feelings wherever this takes us, we come into a new, more compassionate relationship to our lost, rejected, hurting parts, and our suppressed self-expression or power. By engaging in this self-healing practice, we feel empowered to confront painful realities in the world around us rather than avoiding these out of our generalized fear of discomfort. We learn to embody the whole-making process that is our natural evolutionary destiny.

Wholeness is where a life well and consciously lived will take us. When we live in harmony with the laws of life — whether we call this God, the Tao, the Divine, Great Spirit, True Nature, Designing Intelligence, or something else — our personal power gets amplified by joining forces with life's natural laws. This may be the paradigm shift that life is nudging us toward. What first appears as a cascade of unsolvable problems, problems that threaten to overwhelm our capacity to cope, upon further examination can be the gateway to hidden potentials that naturally emerge when we fully face and inquire into the painful reality we thought would overwhelm us.

The Hero's Journey

One lesson from ancient myths about the hero's journey is that every human life, your life, has a contribution to make to the whole. In this life, slings and arrows will come at you. How you live your life affects the whole. The hero's job is to use whatever challenges life serves up to refine the inner and outer seeing and way of being, so that eventually each of us reaches the mountaintop and sees how our one life is insepa- rable from life itself — how I am part of all, and all is in me. The hero achieves this by going into the underworld of the unconscious mind and learning how to make the unconscious conscious.

If your outer life gets too disconnected from the inner, or from the wholeness that you are part of, life will do what it does to get your attention — often by creating painful circum- stances in your outer world. Any time you get out of balance, life will only allow this for so long before it finds a way to restore balance. If you get too grandiose and self-centered (as industrialized nations have gotten with respect to the natural world), life will bring you down to size. If, like Jim, you try to be too forceful and cocky, and deny your frightened, needy, vulnerable side, life will present you with challenges that bring you to your knees. The idea here is that true strength and wis- dom, the kind that enable us to cope with the complexity of today's world situation, require integrated input from all parts of the system, including the vulnerable parts. If some parts are offline, repressed, suppressed, or denied, the resulting action will be less effective.

Trigger reactions are one way life has for getting us to pay attention to what we have been denying. So, also, are world crises. It takes a crisis to get our attention. It is also true that today's problems seem so vast and complex that we instinc- tively want to look the other way. This is true whether we are talking about world problems, like the climate crisis and poverty, or inner problems, like unhealed personal trauma and emotional stress.

Many people are paralyzed to one degree or another by the fear of emotional pain — the pain of the disowned, neglected, frightened child inside. In my life's work, I have seen real transformation happen in people after they do the inner work of healing their fear of pain (which includes the fear of feeling powerless or not in control). When the outer world situation upsets us, now life has our attention. And when we develop the habit of using such upsets to explore our inner world, embracing and therefore *accepting* whatever unpleasant realities we find, now we have more internal resilience. We can bounce back more quickly from disappointments and upsets. We don't get stuck in paralysis, inaction, or reaction. We know how to stay engaged and curious in the face of painful realities (both inner and outer). Armed with a set of skills for doing inner work, we know how to work with the slings and arrows of life. In these chaotic times, too many humans cannot accept *what is*. They waste too much energy focusing on what should or should not be happening versus what is happening. This sets them against seeing and dealing with *what is* and working with their actual reality. Trigger work teaches us to put our attention and energy where they can do some good. We learn to have an I-thou dialogue with unfamiliar or scary parts of ourselves and the world. Instead of building protective walls or aggressive arsenals, we open our attention, get curious, and inquire.

People who once avoided inconvenient truths get really interested in knowing more and learning more. People who once tended to oversimplify problems, seeing things in either-or terms, are able to step outside and above "the level of the problem," get a wide-angle view on things, see how all the parts of a complex system can work together, and create solutions from a both-and or many-sided perspective. Many of us do not realize how complex or many-sided we are — until we begin the work of discovering the many sides or layers of our own beingness hidden away in the shadows of our psyches. Trigger work is the path to owning our many-sidedness and the inner and outer power that comes with this. What we thought would overwhelm us becomes our superpower. This is the work of managing complexity — creating systems (including our internal self-system) where all our parts see one another, communicate with one another, know one another, and care about one another.

We live in stressful times. World problems are more complex than the human mind can comprehend (at our current level of consciousness). But life has given us what we need to address this complexity. It is hidden within our own subconscious minds. Those who have the courage to explore there will hold the key to humanity's future.

Conclusion

In this book, I hope I have opened your eyes to the profound benefits of trigger work. I hope you have seen how you can become inwardly stronger and more resilient by owning that you sometimes feel small and bewildered; how denying any part of yourself ultimately weakens you because when you try to avoid or deny a painful reality, that is when you lose your power to effectively deal with it.

I hope you have seen that a good life is not necessarily a pain-free life and how the pain is so much easier to bear when you attend to it rather than turning your back on it.

I hope you recognize how blaming someone for your upset feelings prevents you from taking responsibility for your wounds and deficits. These wounds are a part of your personal hero's journey. They are not your fault, but since they have shown up in your life, they are yours to deal with. A blaming attitude will prevent you from learning what you need to learn to heal your wounds.

I hope you have a better understanding of how the ego-mind operates to protect you from things you don't need protection from — things like uncertainty, discomfort, and appearing weak, needy, or imperfect — and how this part of the mind tries to control things you really have little or no control over. I hope you are learning to step back from your automatic thinking habits and to remind yourself that this part of the mind comes from how you learned to cope with unmet childhood needs. It is what we might call *the conditioned mind* or *your conditioning.* The aim of the hero's journey is to get free of your childhood conditioning so you can make adult choices based on what is actually happening — instead of what you fear will happen because it happened when you were a child.

I hope you are convinced that pausing frequently to be aware of your inner state is a good practice. Mindfulness breaks like this are beneficial even when you are not triggered, and they could help reduce triggering episodes. When you make pausing a part of your daily life, you give your nervous system time to become calm and your senses time to become open. The result is a more spacious and perceptive field of awareness — you can see more of current reality at once, and you can better "see things coming." Thus, you will experience fewer unwanted surprises.

Pausing also strengthens your capacity for self-witnessing. As you take the position of the witness, you become less identified with the conditioned mind that tends to think something is wrong with you if you feel upset. From the witness perspective, any feeling can be welcomed and held. The witness is that big spacious presence that welcomes everything that's real. It allows you to tenderly hold your pain while at the same time knowing that this pain is not your essential self.

The witness allows you to experience and hold emotional pain while not being identified with the pain.

We live in uncertain, complex, and often overwhelming times. To cope well with the challenges we face, humans need to develop and use more of our potential. The main thing holding us back from such development is our normal, but unnecessary, fear of discomfort or resistance to change. Development takes effort. It is uncomfortable. Doing trigger work teaches us not to avoid uncomfortable feelings. We learn that when we embrace our tender pains and fears, a natural healing process is set in motion. This expands the size of the world we can comfortably and competently deal with. We discover a new relationship with the parts of ourselves that we had believed were the cause of our distress. As it turns out, *denying them* was the cause of our distress. These are the kinds of lessons that come from doing trigger work. We learn that we really do have what it takes to cope with inconvenient truths and unwanted surprises. The world needs more of us who can help lead the way.

About the Author

Susan Campbell received her PhD in clinical psychology from University of Massachusetts in 1967. Since then she has been a couple therapist, relationship coach, speaker, workshop leader, and trainer of professional coaches. She has written eleven previous books on relationships. She started the couple and family therapy graduate training program at UMass and has been a frequent guest faculty at Harvard, Stanford, and UCLA.

Susan trains coaches and therapists to integrate the tools in this book into their professional practices. In her own practice, she works with singles, couples, coworkers, and work teams, helping them communicate respectfully and responsibly when conflicts arise. She works from the model that all significant relationships can be a path for inner growth and healing. Her groundbreaking book, *The Couples Journey: Intimacy as a Path to Wholeness*, published in 1980, was the first popular book that introduced the idea of relationship as a spiritual practice into the mainstream.

She is the creator and publisher of three entertaining and educational card games for teens, adults, couples, work teams, and singles. All of her games promote more authentic relating among players. Susan has appeared on numerous talk shows, including CNN's *News Night*, *Good Morning America*, and *The Dr. Dean Edell Show*, and she has been published widely in popular magazines. In 2003–2004, she was the couple therapist on the reality TV show *Truth in Love*, which aired on UPN, an ABC affiliate network.

Her learning/discovery approach to communication, conflict, and change is the subject of a twenty-minute professional training film produced and distributed by CRM Learning. Based on her book *From Chaos to Confidence: Survival Strategies for the New Workplace*, the film and accompanying workbook are widely used by Fortune 500 companies and government agencies. As an internationally known professional speaker, she speaks to corporate audiences on such topics as "Surfing Chaos," "Honest Feedback in the Workplace," "Coping with Constant Change," "Dealing with Difficult People," and "How to Build a Winning Team." She publishes a free newsletter/blog, which you can subscribe to by visiting her website, www.susancampbell.com.

Susan leads public seminars throughout the United States and in Europe on such topics as "From Triggered to Tranquil," "Rapid Relationship Repair," "Getting Real Confidence," "Conscious Communication," "Truth in Dating," "Truth at Work," "What to Do When Love Hurts," and "The Couple's Journey: Relationship as a Path to Awakening." She has a phone, Zoom, and in-person relationship coaching practice in Sonoma County, California. Susan trains and certifies professional Getting Real coaches to offer her unique brand of coaching and group facilitation. She also hosts couples who come to her home for an entire weekend for an intensive immersion experience using the tools in this book. For more, visit www.susancampbell.com.